T5-BBV-752

When a Woman Takes God at His Word

Kelly —

May this book
enhance your
love for His Word!

Pat Baker

When a Woman Takes God at His Word

PAT BAKER

Tyndale House
Publishers, Inc.
Wheaton, Illinois

Bible Translation Abbreviations

Amp.—The Amplified Bible
Bas.—The New Testament in Basic English
Beck—The Holy Bible in the Language of Today
  (William F. Beck)
Gspd.—The New Testament: An American
  Translation (Edgar J. Goodspeed)
KJV—Holy Bible: King James Version
Mof.—The Bible: A New Translation (James
  Moffatt)
NASB—New American Standard Bible
NEB—The New English Bible
NIV—Holy Bible: New International Version
Phillips—The New Testament in Modern English
  (J. B. Phillips)
Rhm.—The Emphasized Bible (J. B. Rotherham)
RSV—Holy Bible: Revised Standard Version
TEV—Good News Bible: Today's English Version
Wey.—The New Testament in Modern Speech
  (Richard F. Weymouth)
Wms.—The New Testament in the Language of
  the People (Charles B. Williams)

Permission to quote from the following sources
has been granted by each publisher.
Matthew Henry's One-Volume Commentary by
Matthew Henry. Copyright © 1960 by Marshall,
Morgan and Scott; copyright © 1961 by
Zondervan Publishing House. "My Experiment
with Fault Finding" by Catherine Marshall, March
1983 *Guideposts* magazine. Copyright © 1983 by
Guideposts Associates, Inc.
    Unless otherwise noted all Scripture is taken
from *The Living Bible.* Copyright © 1971 by
Tyndale House Publishers.

Second printing, June 1988

Library of Congress Catalog Card Number 86-50923
ISBN 0-8423-7975-4
Copyright © 1986 by Pat Baker
All rights reserved
Printed in the United States of America

To the thirty-one women who prayed for me as I wrote this book and rejoiced with me when it was finished

Thank you:

Doris Card and Linda Smith Tappmeyer for correcting misspelled words, deleting split infinitives, rearranging paragraphs, and improving sentence structure in the final draft of this manuscript

Dr. Gordon Dutile, Greek scholar extraordinaire, for not asking me to return the many books on loan from his personal library while I was writing this book

Dr. Claude Mariottini, respected Hebrew scholar, for helping me use Old Testament words in their proper contexts

and

Don, my husband, for giving up many of his Saturday mornings and noon hours to help me pull from my mind and heart how I wanted to express these precious truths from God's Word.

CONTENTS

PREFACE:

Stepping into Faith & Obedience

I have changed in many ways since I started writing this book. I have compared some of those changes to an event that occurred in Joshua 3.

The scene:
> It was the harvest season and the Jordan was overflowing all its banks (v. 14).

It was the season in my life when I wanted to write another book but couldn't decide what to write. Late that fall I was listening to an evangelist who kept repeating, "All you have to do is take God at his Word." I made a notation of the sentence. I began to search the Scriptures and to ask myself over and over, "Do I really believe what I read in the Scriptures? *Do* I take God at his Word?"

The command:
> When you see the priests carrying the Ark of God, follow them. You have never before been where we are going now, so they will guide you. . . . Tomorrow . . . the Lord will do a

great miracle. . . . When the priests who are
carrying the Ark touch the water with their
feet, the river will stop flowing as though
held back by a dam, and will pile up as
though against an invisible wall! (vv. 3, 5, 13).

In response to this example of faith, I believed
that God was directing me to write this book. I had
no idea what it would involve.

Faith required:

As the feet of the priests who were carrying
the Ark touched the water at the river's edge,
suddenly, far up the river . . . the water began
piling up as though against a dam! (vv. 14b,
15).

With faith, I took the first steps toward writing
this book. I had a nearly perfect plan that I
believed would allow me to finish the writing in
four months. When the fifth month began and
the book was still in its early stages, I became
frustrated. I wondered if God had commanded me
to write the book. In my frustration, God gave me
direction through Hebrews 11:1, 2.

What is faith? It is the confident assurance
that something we want is going to happen. It
is the certainty that what we hope for is
waiting for us, even though we cannot see it
up ahead. Men of God in days of old were
famous for their faith.

For several days I contemplated the faith of
many godly people throughout the Scriptures:
Abraham, Sarah, Noah, Esther.
I witnessed the faith of Peter when Jesus told

him to lay down the earthly possessions that provided his livelihood.

I wondered how Moses felt when God told him to lay down his rod. God knew how important that rod was to Moses, but he demanded that Moses let go of it.

God used another woman as his instrument to tell me to lay down my writing. I balked. I didn't want to give it up. It was important to me; and besides, I had accepted this assignment as a commission from God. In faith, not knowing what was "up ahead," I obeyed and laid down the manuscript.

Obedience rewarded:

> . . . and the priests who were carrying the Ark stood on dry ground in the middle of the Jordan and waited as all the people passed by (Josh. 3:17).

In obedience, the priests had stepped into the flood before there was any evidence that the waters were going to part.

In obedience, Peter laid down his nets and went on to become a fisherman for the souls of men.

In obedience, Moses obeyed God. He picked up his rod and it became the rod of God. He was then able to set God's people free!

I picked up my book one month after I had laid it down. There had been no evidence that God would ask me to pick it up again, but he did!

The priests stepped into that flooded river because they had faith in God's command and were obedient to it. My commission was different, but the completion of this book also depended on my faith and obedience to God.

Postscript. I know there will still be times when I may not understand what God wants to teach me.

Some of his commands will tell me to go beyond what I believe I'm capable of doing, but that's when faith will take me beyond human reasoning.

He will continue to command me to lay down those things that have become too important to me. This command may seem impossible, but I must trust God and be obedient to what he has commanded me to do.

I invite you to step with me into this ongoing journey of faith and obedience through God's Word.

Pat Baker

INTRODUCTION

Congratulations! You have chosen one of the most practical books you'll ever read, a book that tells you what can happen when you start taking God at his Word.

Possibly you have spent countless hours searching for ways to get the most out of life but have wound up in blind alleys and on one-way streets. You will never be fully satisfied until you stop bypassing the main source. *The lasting answers for a life full of purpose are found in God's Word.*

Because you have selected this book, you are ready to experience some of the most exciting, profitable times of your life. The fact that you were attracted to this book's title is evidence that you're ready to start taking God at his Word.

About This Book
The Purpose:
1. To intensify your love for God's Word.
2. To introduce six special truths to enhance your Christian life.

3. To encourage you to apply the six truths.
The Plan:
You can participate in seven one-hour discussion sessions with other Christian women or use the book for individual study.
The Procedure:
1. Read one chapter per week.
2. A self-evaluation section, "Confronting Yourself," follows each chapter. Think about each activity before you write your answers.
3. Write your answers. Have this section completed before your discussion group meets. These activities give you the opportunity to share with other women how God reveals specific truths about himself and your life. You will hear other women share how their lives are being steadily changed through this study.
4. The "Stretching Exercises" following your self-evaluation include Scripture verses to be read daily.

What This Book Has for You. The six chapters in this book pinpoint six special truths from God's Word. The first truth alerts you to the importance of a daily Bible study time.

The next truth involves three basic Christian concepts, a game plan, and a command from God.

Through a confirmation of the Scriptures, God teaches in the third truth the benefits of waiting on and listening to him.

The fourth truth explains that you may be walking through your Christian life with unnecessary guilt. This special truth involves learning how to accept God's kind of forgiveness.

The fifth truth helps you accept your body as God made it and admit that God has also created within you abilities he wants you to discover and use to bring honor to him.

The final special truth informs you of the beautiful life of ministry you'll have as you take God at his Word.

Confronting Yourself

(Use with the first discussion period. Or answer the questions that apply to your individual study. If you are in a group with more than ten women, divide into smaller groups for the longer activities.)

I. As far as your spiritual needs are concerned:
   A. What do you need/want to learn from this book?

   B. What do you need/want to learn from the group discussions?

II. Before you start discussing the book, meditate on this verse: "Our goal is to measure up to God's plan for us" (2 Cor. 10:13).

   Join hands. Pray and commit to God: the next seven weeks of study; the place where you will be meeting; and each woman attending.

III. Based on the six special truths outlined in the introduction, on a scale of 0-10, estimate where you are in your spiritual growth process and knowledge of the Scriptures. Circle the appropriate number.

0 - 1 - 2 - 3 - 4 - 5 - 6 - 7 - 8 - 9 - 10

Not	Very
Good	Good

Then put a check by the number you hope to reach by the time this book is completed.
A. The number you circled says:

B. The number you checked says:

C. Using the second number, share your aspirations with the group.

IV. This activity is to be done in groups of twos or threes. Write out your answers if you are studying alone. (These verses describe the six special truths that will be discussed in this book.) What truths is God teaching in these Scripture verses?
A. "Thy words were found and I ate them, and Thy words became for me a joy and the delight of my

heart" (Jer. 15:16, NASB).
TRUTH:

B. "Everything else is worthless when compared with the priceless gain of knowing Christ Jesus my Lord" (Phil. 3:8).
TRUTH:

C. "Be patient and wait for the Lord to act" (Ps. 37:7, TEV).
TRUTH:

D. "The more we see our sinfulness, the more we see God's abounding grace forgiving us" (Rom. 5:20).
TRUTH:

E. ". . . glorify God in your body" (1 Cor. 6:20, RSV).
   TRUTH:

F. "God has given each of us the ability to do certain things well" (Rom. 12:6a).
   TRUTH:

G. "For God sees not as man sees, for man looks at the outward appearance, but the Lord looks at the heart" (1 Sam. 16:7b, NASB).
   TRUTH:

Which truth do you find the easiest to take God at his Word?

Which truth do you have the most difficulty accepting? What makes it difficult?

This week, memorize the Scripture verse you have the most difficulty accepting. Read it from different translations. Discover the key word and meditate on it. Share any new insights with the group next week.

V. Share with one other person a verse in God's Word on which you have come to rely. If appropriate, tell what circumstances make it *your* verse.

VI. What is your greatest spiritual need? Resolve, with God's help, to work on meeting that need.
RESOLVE:

VII. As the session ends:
   A. Silently tell God your needs.
   B. Believe God has heard you.
   C. Be ready to receive from God whatever it is you need in your spiritual growth process.

S T R E T C H I N G
E X E R C I S E S

*The verses in this special section following
each chapter will stretch you spiritually.*

1. *Before you read a verse, make this request to God:
   "Open my eyes to see wonderful things in your Word"
   (Ps. 119:18).*
2. *Read one verse each day.*
3. *Ask yourself: "What did I hear God saying in this
   verse?"*
4. *Meditate on this truth three times during the day.*
5. *The Advanced Stretching Exercises are to be repeated
   daily until they are memorized.*

1
Spiritual Veils

I have no choice except to start this book with the most essential truth of all: I acknowledge the incomparable power of God's Word and affirm the life transformation that occurs when I read and study his Word daily.

After I accepted this truth, I looked forward to incorporating Scripture reading and study into my daily schedule. This habit brought me into greater understanding and awareness of God. One morning as I read the story of the crucifixion from the Gospel of Matthew, I came to the part where the temple veil tore from top to bottom at Jesus' death. That incident intrigued me. I pictured the veil to be like the heavy velvet curtains I had seen hanging across high school stages.

Then I researched the history of the veil and learned that it was one solid piece of material made of beautiful fine-spun linen. The only people who were allowed to go beyond the veil were the temple priests. Later, this access was limited to the

High Priest who went behind the veil only once a year on the Day of Atonement. At the precise moment of Jesus' death, the veil split from top to bottom. The most Holy Place was now exposed to everyone.

The gospel story conveyed the message that I could have as much access to God as I wanted. It made me aware that, until that point, I had not gone before God nearly enough to acquire an in-depth relationship with him through his Word. My own spiritual veil had to tear in two in order to expose more of God. This happened, in God's timing, as surely as it did that day when he willed the veil in the temple to tear in two.

BEFORE MY VEIL TORE IN TWO

I first started reading God's Word every day so that I could check the square designated "Daily Bible Reading" on my church offering envelope. When that challenge wore off, I only read the Scriptures when it was convenient. During some of those times I read several verses and even chapters at one sitting. I skipped over the books of Leviticus and Numbers because the laws and long lists of "begats" were monotonous. Very few passages in the Old Testament seemed to relate to my life, but I kept reading.

It would be several years before I would begin to "thirst" for the Scriptures. First I spent many years busily working on my college education and searching for a husband. After succeeding at both goals, over the next several years I became the mother of three daughters. Parenting managed to take up most of my time.

I wanted to be a good mother. "Good" meant persevering through three bouts of chicken pox,

attending piano recitals, standing in subzero
temperatures as the girls marched in parades,
waiting for them to come home from their dates,
and helping each one get ready for her wedding
day. Not always, but many times, my motive for
reading the Bible was to set a good example for the
children.

During those busy years my personal relationship
with God was real, but my knowledge about him
was vague. I rationalized why I hadn't spent more
time in the Scriptures: "I can't be expected to know
as much about the Bible as ministers and Bible
professors. Part of their job is to study the
Scriptures and share their findings with me.
Besides, my days are completely occupied with
being a good mother." Rationalizing soon began to
make me "deaf to the words of God."

To take some breaks from parenting, I became
involved in social clubs and church programs. My
activities were constructive, but did not lead to a
love for the Scriptures. I had no way of knowing
how I would be taught submission to God's Word.
My spiritual veil was about to tear and I was to
realize soon that it would involve one of my
children.

As each of our daughters was born, my husband
and I dedicated her to God. But the longer we lived
together as a family, the more I began to try to
reclaim that gift. One evening after an explosive
scene with one of our teens, God convicted me and
I realized that I was trying to hold onto my
daughters. It was time to give them back to him.
Self-sufficient me, with all the virtues that go with
natural parental instincts—I was being told by God
to give up exactly what was giving me purpose and
making me feel useful.

I relinquished my daughters to God after a long

night of spiritual struggle. I submitted to God's
Word: "Everything I have comes from you
(daughters included) and I am giving you back
what is yours already" (paraphrased from 1 Chron.
29:14). I gave my daughters *and* myself back to
him that night.

Years before I had given my life and my
children's lives to God. Now I was being asked to
continue to trust him with our lives. I had spent
many years "being a good mother," but now the
time was ripe for me to enter another role that
would deepen my personal relationship with God
through the Scriptures.

MY VEIL TEARS IN TWO

With the release of my children and myself to God,
the next phase involved reading and studying the
Scriptures more diligently. Until that time, I had
heard hundreds of sermons that emphasized the
importance of reading and studying the Bible. Some
of the sermons were so stimulating that I'd go
home from church and read the Bible faithfully
each day for almost a week. Then my enthusiasm
would let up until I heard another motivating
sermon.

Some of my friends, who were as busy as I, tried
to convince me that having a regular time each day
to read the Bible and pray would help me enjoy life
more, enable me to have a higher tolerance toward
other people, and actually uncomplicate my busy
life. The last reason made sense.

One morning, shortly after the night when I
released my children and myself back to the Lord,
I made a serious commitment to God: "I will
give three minutes a day to reading your Word

and praying. If I notice any change in my life after a month, I will continue this commitment indefinitely."

That same day I read a portion of Scripture for one minute and I prayed for two minutes. As I prayed, I kept glancing at my watch to make sure I didn't go over the two minutes. My loving, patient Lord must have been saying, "This poor woman needs help!"

There have been some obvious changes in my life since that commitment. I no longer look at my watch while I'm reading the Scriptures and praying. With the psalmist, I have begun to "open my eyes to see wonderful things in his Word. I admit I am but a pilgrim here on earth. How I need a map—and God's commands are my chart and guide. I long for his instructions more than I can tell" (paraphrased from Ps. 119:18, 19).

I spent each morning carrying out my commitment. I recorded my thoughts about certain Scripture verses in my daily journal. Eventually these thoughts were reproduced in a devotional book.

As the book was completed I noticed that each devotional thought took approximately three minutes to read. I encouraged the readers to contemplate one devotional thought each day and see if some changes would occur in their lives by the time they finished reading the book. If they noticed that some changes had occurred because they had specifically met God three minutes each day, I suggested that they commit the remainder of their lives to reading the Scriptures daily. The work God can do in a person's life, when even three minutes a day are allotted to him, continually amazes me.

For years I followed various Bible reading plans, but no plan instructed me to stop at a given word within a verse and saturate myself with its meaning, a practice I now found myself doing. The more I read the Scriptures the more I wanted to learn. Psalm 42:1 described my desire to learn: "As a deer pants for water, so I long for you, O God." I asked Bible professors at a local university to help explain certain verses. They loaned me their word study books, commentaries, and concordances. I borrowed or bought other Bible translations, poring over many of the words as though I had never seen them before. I meditated on some words for days, even as I shopped and waited in lines at grocery stores and performed other household duties. When I wasn't reading them or saying them aloud, they interrupted my thoughts.

I experienced a new love for the Scriptures. It started with reading God's Word regularly and expectantly, three minutes a day. The Holy Spirit then began to reveal more of God's truths to me. In the process I discovered a Scripture verse that expressed my new love: "Thy words were found and I ate them, and Thy words became for me a joy and the delight of my heart" (Jer. 15:16, NASB).

My spiritual veil had torn in two. There had been no earthly coercion, no pharisaical motive in my decision to start reading and studying the Scriptures regularly. I simply desired to deepen my relationship with God, and it began to happen through the study of the Scriptures.

Before my spiritual veil tore in two, I had never taken time to become acquainted with such love, such compassion and forgiveness as only God could give me.

MY NEXT STEP

As I stayed with my commitment to read and study the Scriptures regularly, God led me out of full-time parenting and into a new line of work. The new occupation involved a ministry of writing. Parenting became a part-time job simply because my daughters were older and didn't need me as much as they had earlier. My extra hours now became filled with writing. The girls' reaction? They were *so* relieved! They were finding new roles also, learning how to function in an adult world without parents constantly overseeing their activities.

I set aside three hours a day to write, which meant that the schedule I had kept for years had to be revised. Until I started writing I thought almost every woman in America, even if she worked outside her home, had a fixed schedule of shopping for groceries on Thursday, cleaning her house on Friday, and washing on Saturday. But I no longer felt regimented to this schedule. If I was busy writing, I sometimes didn't go to the grocery store on the assigned day; however, my family still had their regular meals each day. I took shortcuts in my housecleaning and found that if I did the washing a day other than Saturday, everyone still had clean outfits to wear on Sunday.

This new approach was not devoid of anxious moments. There were times when I doubted that God ever wanted me to write. But those experiences caused me to spend more time reading and studying the Scriptures, allowing me to receive new insights, direction, and assurance. Philippians 1:6 became my reassurance verse: "God who began the good work within you will keep right on helping you grow in his grace until his task within

you is finally finished." I continue to commit my
work to God on a daily basis, and he continues to
help me.

I have placed this prayer on my bulletin board
directly above my typewriter as a daily reminder of
God's promise to me and my promise to him.

> Lord, I dedicate this work to you. I come to
> you first, asking you to guide me in it. My
> sole purpose is to bring honor to the One who
> has given me the ability to do this work.
> I yield myself to your control. When I do
> this I know the Holy Spirit is provided with
> the opportunity he needs to transform my life
> and my work to the extent that you will be
> glorified.

I am convinced that the main way to discover
more about God and what he expects of me is to
study his Word daily. This regular habit helps me
be a less anxious, worried, insecure woman who is
now learning to enjoy her spiritual inheritance as
one of God's children.

OTHERS' VEILS

Several years after I made the commitment to read
and study God's Word daily, I became acquainted
with a group of women who had made a similar
commitment. They were faithfully pursuing a
greater understanding of God, but they also wanted
to learn how God was teaching *other* women
through his Word. God honored their desire by
leading them to organize a conference designed
especially for women who needed to hear both how
God was working through other women's lives and
how he could work in their own lives.

The first time these women met to begin making preparations, the coordinator stood and said, "Ladies, there's no way we can pull off this conference by ourselves." Before anything else was done they prayed that God would lead them. God led these women to claim this portion of his Word: "Every place that the sole of your foot shall tread upon, that have I given unto you" (Josh. 1:3, KJV). This promise assured them that the presence of God would be with them as they made necessary preparations for the conference. Each time they met, their plans were touched either by the promises from God's Word or by prayer.

They continued to claim Joshua 1:3 as they literally walked through the entire church building, committing it to God. They stood around the piano, organ, pulpit, and sound booth, committing each one of them to God. They prayed for each person who would be standing or sitting at each of those places. They sat in each pew and workshop area and prayed by name for each woman who had registered to come.

One thousand women responded to the conference invitation. Toward the end of the meetings the women were asked to fill out evaluation forms. The following comments demonstrate the impact the conference had on their lives.

> Because of this conference, my marriage has been saved.

> This has been a time when God has pulled me apart into little pieces and has started putting me together again to conform to his image.

> It's been so good to be with Jesus. I've climbed one step higher.

I feel like I'm worth something for the first time in my life.

When I came to this conference, I had decided that if I didn't find some answers and a purpose for living, I would end my life. But I have found my purpose.

These evaluations expressed the renewal of women's minds and their realization of the Holy Spirit's power to change lives. Such decisions were made because a group of women claimed a promise that God's presence would lead them through their preparations and the conference itself.

I knew personally that the Holy Spirit had arrived at the conference long before I did. He stayed during the conference and his influence went with the women as they left. I can't speak for all of them, but I can say that the Spirit's influence during those hours is still with me.

YOUR VEIL

You are the only one who knows how close or how far away you are from acting upon the first truth of reading and studying the Scriptures daily. Maybe you are asking the same question I asked before I accepted the importance of this truth: "Why do I keep searching in other places for truth when God teaches that I can find *perfect truth* only in his Word?"

I searched many other places to find the truth before I turned to the Scriptures. The books on my shelves looked as though I had purchased at least one of each title claiming to give me the answers about how to stay in love with my husband, how to discipline my children, how to feel better about myself, and how to pray. I also purchased tapes in my search—but reading books and listening to tapes weren't enough. I went to church, listened to sermons, attended Bible studies, retreats, and prayer groups. As I received study awards and hung them on an obscure wall in the utility room, I *still* wondered if I had gained any truths that would last.

God *does* use other people to teach us about his Word—ministers, Bible teachers, authors. These people motivate us, inspire us, and challenge our minds to learn more. It's also helpful to observe "outstanding" Christians. But when God says "whosoever," he's saying that not only outstanding Christians have access to truths about him—*so do the rest of us.* Neither do these "spiritual achievers" (and I use the term respectfully) own special limited editions of the Bible with verses that aren't in ours. We don't have to always depend on someone else to teach us scriptural truths. We can have as much access to God as we want to have. That truth was revealed the day the temple veil tore in two.

There are two basic steps to follow in the first special truth: Read and study the Scriptures regularly and have confidence that the Holy Spirit will teach you truths that last!

❀ Confronting Yourself

I. What insights did you gain last week from the verse with which you had the most difficulty?

II. Share the part of this chapter that gave you something new to think about.

III. Prepare a brief statement describing how you feel about God's Word.

IV. Check the answer that best describes your schedule:
   A. How often do you read the Scriptures?
      ___daily ___weekly ___monthly ___holidays/
                                              vacations

B. How often do you *study* the Scriptures (using commentaries, etc.)?

___daily ___weekly ___monthly ___holidays/vacations

C. How many minutes per day/week do you read the Scriptures?

___5 ___10 ___15 ___30 ___more

D. When do you read the Scriptures?

___morning ___afternoon ___night

E. How would you evaluate the time you spend reading the Scriptures?

___inspiring ___great ___good ___so-so

Which checks show your most needy area?

_____

V. Which day of the week is the busiest?
Make a "Where Does the Day Go?" list. List every activity in which you are involved that day.

Write a 1 by each activity you *must do.* Write a 2 by the activities you *enjoy.* Write a 3 by the other activities you feel *locked into* but haven't figured out how to drop. (Make sure every activity has a number by it.) *The objective:* Drop one of the number 3s. Use the time involved with that activity for regular Bible study. *Tell the group which activity you can drop to reach your objective.*

VI. Dialogue with one other person. Have a small photo of someone, or an object to represent something you haven't released to God. (Example: A clock to represent your time.) Discuss this with each other.
A. Repeat this verse together. "[Who are we] that we should be permitted to give anything to [God]? Everything we have has come from [him], and we only give [him] what is [his] already" (1 Chron. 29:14).

B. How does this verse apply to you when it comes to releasing everything to God?

VII. Find and list four truths about God from the Scriptures.
For starters:
A. "What a glorious Lord! He who daily bears our burdens also gives us our salvation. He frees us! He rescues us from death" (Ps. 68:19, 20).

B.

C.

D.

E.

Share one truth about God with the group.

Share one word that describes how knowing that truth makes you feel.

_____

VIII. Draw up a resolution in light of this study today. (This will be referred to in the last group session.) *RESOLVE:*

S T R E T C H I N G
E X E R C I S E S

*Open my eyes to see wonderful things in
your Word.*

FIRST DAY:
*"Now, when sins have once been forever forgiven and
forgotten, there is no need to offer more sacrifices to get
rid of them. And so, dear brothers, now we may walk
right into the very Holy of Holies where God is, because
of the blood of Jesus. This is the fresh, new, life-giving
way which Christ has opened up for us by tearing the
curtain—his human body—to let us into the holy
presence of God" (Heb. 10:18-20).*

SECOND DAY:
*"God's laws are perfect. They protect us, make us wise,
and give us joy and light. God's laws are pure, eternal,
just. They are more desirable than gold. They are
sweeter than honey dripping from a honeycomb. For they
warn us away from harm and give success to those who
obey them" (Ps. 19:7-11).*

THIRD DAY:
*"Remember what Christ taught and let his words enrich
your lives and make you wise" (Col. 3:16).*

FOURTH DAY:
*"Those who love your laws have great peace of heart and
mind and do not stumble. . . . I have looked for your
commandments and I love them very much; yes, I have*

*searched for them. You know this because everything I
do is known to you" (Ps. 119:165, 167, 168).*

FIFTH DAY:
*"The sum of your Word is truth (the total of the full
meanings of all your individual precepts) and every one
of your righteous decrees endures for ever" (Ps.
119:160, Amp.).*

SIXTH DAY:
*"As the rain and snow come down from heaven and stay
upon the ground to water the earth, and cause the grain
to grow and to produce seed for the farmer and bread
for the hungry, so also is my Word. I send it out and it
always produces fruit. It shall accomplish all I want it to,
and prosper everywhere I send it" (Isa. 55:10, 11).*

SEVENTH DAY:
*"The whole Bible was given to us by inspiration from God
and is useful to teach us what is true and to make us
realize what is wrong in our lives; it straightens us out
and helps us do what is right. It is God's way of making
us well prepared at every point, fully equipped to do
good to everyone" (2 Tim. 3:16, 17).*

ADVANCED STRETCHING EXERCISE
*"For the word that God speaks is alive and active . . . it
strikes through to the place where soul and spirit meet,
to the innermost intimacies of man's being: it examines
the very thoughts and motives of a man's heart" (Heb.
4:12, Phillips).*

2
Getting Back to Spiritual Basics

Several months into the first truth of reading and studying the Scriptures daily, I looked back over some of the verses I had underlined in my Bible, plus those I had recorded in my daily journal, and a light came on. I called it "the illumination of the Holy Spirit." Those Scripture verses cleared up many questions that had bothered me through the years. Through them, the Holy Spirit revealed three spiritual concepts that became the basis of my Christian beliefs. I could consider the awesomeness of God's Master Plan in smaller segments. I could see that the Christian life isn't impossible, and that the highest standards are attainable with God's help.

As I pondered these basic concepts, I began to branch out into a study of other teachings in the Scriptures. But I noticed that each new truth, directly or indirectly, related back to these three basic concepts.

Basic Concept One: You Were Created for the Purpose of Praising and Glorifying God.
This first concept is outlined in Ephesians 1:

> Long ago, even before he made the world, God chose us to be his very own, through what Christ would do for us; he decided then to make us holy in his eyes, without a single fault—we who stand before him covered with his love. His unchanging plan has always been to adopt us into his own family by sending Jesus Christ to die for us. And he did this because he wanted to!
>
> God has told us his secret reason for sending Christ, a plan he decided on in mercy long ago; and this was his purpose: that when the time is ripe he will gather us all together from wherever we are—in heaven or on earth—to be with him in Christ, forever . . . and all things happen just as he decided long ago. GOD'S PURPOSE IN THIS WAS THAT WE SHOULD PRAISE GOD AND GIVE GLORY TO HIM for doing these mighty things for us . . . (Eph. 1:4, 5, 9-12).

This concept instructed me that God's children are to live in such a way that they bring attention to him through their lives. It completely discourages the ever-present temptation to draw attention to self.

Genesis 29:35 ("I will *praise* the Lord"), to Revelation 4:11 ("O Lord, you are worthy to receive the *glory* and the *honor* and the power, for you have created all things"), and many pages in between, teach that God is the only One who deserves praise.

"All who claim me as their God will come, for I have made them for my *glory*" (Isa. 43:7).

Basic Concept Two: You Were Created for the Purpose of Pleasing God.
The words "please" and "pleasure" are recorded throughout the Bible, and they enforce the basic concept of pleasing God. When this concept is included in your Christian beliefs you lay yourself wide open to learn through the Scriptures *what* pleases him.

God tells you that it pleases him when you "love your neighbor as yourself"; when you "try hard to live peaceably with everyone"; and when you "pray much and worry less." He's pleased when you're "patient during trying times," and when he sees your life producing the fruits of the Spirit. He's pleased when you hand over anything that concerns you and let him take that "heavy yoke" from you.

God is so in tune with you that he picks up on your daily relationships and incidents, and he's pleased when he sees you carrying out his teachings. This story from the book of Haggai reinforces the basic concept of pleasing God.

After the children of Israel came out of captivity, God told the prophet Haggai to inform them that the first thing they were to do was rebuild the temple. After they had laid the temple's foundation, they stopped working on it and started building their own houses. It wasn't as though they weren't going to get back to building the temple, but they had been gone for a long time and felt that they needed to build their own houses.

Next they planted their crops. With the crops in, they were assured of some income. But a drought came and they lost everything. God asked them,

"Do you know why this happened? *I* caused the drought. I told you that first you were to rebuild my temple *before you did anything else.* But since you ignored my command, I held back from giving my blessings to you."

It's reassuring to learn that God didn't turn his back on the children of Israel because they hadn't pleased him. Instead he "stirred up the spirit . . . of the people; and they came and worked on the house of the Lord of hosts, their God" (Hag. 1:14, NASB).

The concept of pleasing God didn't lose its significance when the Israelites grew old and died. It's an updated truth that can relate to any Christian's life. When you learn to behave in a way that pleases God, he promises that you can "live this life better and better" (1 Thess. 4:10, Wms.).

Basic Concept Three: You Are Created for the Purpose of Developing a Growing Relationship with God.

God has created in you an unparalleled nature, unlike any other part of his creation. You were created to relate to God. This formula helps make God's plan work: Saturate yourself with God by talking with him and studying about him through the Scriptures. This discipline produces a powerful love relationship.

To get this concept across to his congregation, one pastor began an evening service in an unusual way. Without telling anyone, he asked four teenagers to sit in the sound booth, and, at a specified time, to take turns talking over the public address system. Before they started talking, the people in the congregation were instructed to raise their hands as soon as they recognized the voice of each teen. As each of the teens spoke, his or her parents were the first to raise their hands. Their relationship with each other, plus the time they had spent together, helped the parents recognize their teens' voices immediately. That's the kind of relationship God wants to have with you, so that when he speaks you'll recognize his voice (John 10:27).

One mother recognized God's voice during a desperate time in her life. It involved a tragic circumstance concerning her teenage son. To find out how to deal with the situation, she left home, checked into a motel, and stayed for several days. She didn't go back home until she recognized God's voice telling her to keep loving her son, no matter what, in order for him to return to God.

A growing relationship with God gets you so tightly bound up in him that you do what he tells you to do even though you're not sure of the outcome. It happens because you recognize God's voice and follow through with what he says. This kind of relationship has everything to do with how you view life and how you handle it—otherwise the purpose for which God created you gets out of focus.

A professor in a Christian college learned the value of a growing relationship with God years ago. Since then, he spends as much time as necessary teaching its importance to his students. He draws five circles on the chalkboard to resemble a target. On the inside circle, the "bull's eye," he writes "Christian person." He progresses to the outer circles with "marriage," "parent," "church," "employment," and "community." Whether or not the students agree with the priority arrangement of all the circles, it's imperative that they conclude that their personal relationship with God is in the right place.

The effects of a growing relationship with God

carry over into daily incidents. When you get a speeding ticket, or receive too much change back from a clerk, or get a phone call that tears your life in two—you see the difference that a relationship with God makes. It affects you when you're alone or afraid, or driving to the home of a friend whose child has been killed in an accident. It compels you to visit a widow and listen to her talk about her memories. It urges you to be sensitive enough to tell your family that you love them.

This third concept teaches that when a personal relationship with God develops, and only then, do all other human relationships fall into their proper places.

These three concepts are checkpoints that help me determine whether or not I am bringing honor to God, pleasing him, and enhancing my relationship with him. Being aware of these basic concepts, I am more relaxed in the Lord than I've ever been. As my study of the Scriptures continues, I expect the Holy Spirit to reveal other concepts; but for now these three are alive and working well!

A BASIC GAME PLAN

Shortly after I discovered these three basic concepts, I read a Scripture passage, 2 Peter 1:3-8, that included the best basic game plan I had ever come across. It outlined a progressive Christian life-style. The plan followed this order:

1. Get to know God better.
2. Discover what he wants you to do.
3. Learn to put aside your own desires.
4. Enjoy, like, and love other people.

The result of the plan: "You will grow strong spiritually and become fruitful and useful to our Lord Jesus Christ" (v. 8).

After reading this passage from *The Living Bible* and studying each verse, it was my privilege as one of God's "whosoevers" to start to live out the steps that were outlined.

Game Plan: Step One. The first question asked in 2 Peter 1:2 got my attention immediately: "Do you want more and more of God's kindness and peace? Then learn to know him better and better." God not only teaches you to get to know him better, he tells you *why:* "For as you know him better, he will give you, through his great power, everything you need for living a truly good life: he even shares his own glory and his own goodness with us!" (1:3). God is willing to share the spotlight that only he deserves.

The key word in this passage is "know." The definition goes deeper than Webster defines it. The way it is used here, it means more than an intellectual understanding of God.

Years ago an incident happened that later helped me interpret what God was teaching me about getting to *know* him.

The first day I arrived on campus as a college freshman, I noticed a certain young man strutting around campus. I asked an upperclassman if she knew him. She did and immediately began to list his credentials. They sounded impressive, but *I* wasn't impressed.

Several weeks later a friend introduced us to each other. I tolerated the introduction. Later, he asked me for a date. I had an average time. He asked me out again, and that time I enjoyed being with him.

A few months into dating steadily, I started liking him. Within a year the "like" turned into mutual love, and we began to make plans to be married. I hesitate to use the word "addicted" to describe our relationship, because of the word's negative connotations; but during that year we became just that—"addicted" to each other. We felt we couldn't get along without each other. We were so involved in each other's lives that we wanted to commit ourselves to each other, and through our marriage our lives became fused.

This Scripture passage teaches that we are to know God to the degree that we concede we can't get along without him! We become so involved with him that we unite our lives with his. That union begins when we are introduced to him. We like what we hear. We realize that no one else will ever love us more than he loves us. The more we find out, the more we fall in love with God. The love becomes so deep we completely commit our lives to him.

The Scriptures continually draw our attention to the steady, gradual process of knowing God better.

"*Keep on growing* in spiritual knowledge and insight" (Phil. 1:9).

". . . *continually learning* more and more" (Col. 3:10).

"God . . . will *keep right on helping you grow* in his grace" (Phil. 1:6).

The process of getting to know God better takes a long time (a lifetime).

Game Plan: Step Two. When you get to know God better, you will "*discover what he wants you to do*" (2 Pet. 1:5b), rather than being overly concerned with what others expect of you. This in itself leads to a less complicated life.

Instead of being trapped in so many outside involvements, you may learn from this step that God simply wants you to be a better housekeeper and have more time with your husband, children,

or yourself! Sound too unchallenging? Unimportant?
Not if that's what God wants you to do. When you
notice your husband no longer expresses feelings of
neglect, your children stop arguing and kicking
each other under the dinner table, and you have a
more positive concept of yourself, you'll know
you've begun to include this step in your life.

Game Plan: Step Three. "Next, learn to put aside
your own desires" (2 Pet. 1:6a). In the early stages
of my study, I learned that a selfish desire is
nothing more than self-gratification which lasts a
very short time. This knowledge primed me for a
time of painful self-examination.

By nature I'm an organizer, a stickler for details,
and most of the time that's a plus for me. The new
skill that emerged as God taught me to put away
my selfish desires was in the area of flexibility. I
learned to be more flexible in my planning, and
more sensitive to other people's desires, including
those of my family.

As I studied this third step, it became apparent
that I was not considering my husband's desires.
When we ate out, we usually ate where I suggested.
When our children visited us, I was the one who
usually planned what we would do while we were
together. I normally suggested which guests I
wanted to invite for a meal.

I was soon to acknowledge an abundance of
selfish desires that God wanted me to eliminate
from my life.

During a two-hour session that my husband
called after our children had visited us, we had a
meeting of the wills. My husband began telling me
some messages he was receiving from me. First, he
wanted to make sure I understood that he was an
important family member. He mentioned that he'd

occasionally like to suggest whom we might invite as dinner guests. I learned that there were special things he wanted to do when we visited our children. He added that he didn't particularly like my choice of a restaurant all the time.

It's only fair to my husband to say that most of the time he is right in his evaluation of me. Most of the time we understand each other. But in his quiet, loving nature, he had been giving me false messages that my desires were completely acceptable to him.

As he talked, it took immense self-control for me to remain calm. I had the choice of resenting everything he said and of defending my case, or of believing what he said and doing something about it.

I began making a conscious effort to be sensitive to his desires. I didn't keep a running total, but many times I did ask my husband, "Where would *you* like to eat tonight?" "Whom would *you* like to invite as guests?" The responses I got didn't surprise me because I was learning to put aside some of my selfish desires in our relationship. I continue to work at laying aside some of my perfect, well-intentioned plans in our marriage— not always willingly. But I'm trying, especially when I recognize my ideas as selfish desires.

There are hundreds of other selfish desires waiting to consume us. There is one in particular that is prevalent and, sorry to say, acceptable among many women. This desire can develop with an act as innocent as looking through a mail order catalog or going window-shopping. The desire takes shape when we fill in the catalog order blank or when we stop window-shopping and step into our favorite stores. It's the desire for new clothes.

It had always been difficult for me to walk into a

certain clothing store and not come out with a package. Sometimes I would take an article of clothing home on approval, but I knew once I got it to my house it would probably never leave. Other times I bought out of the satisfaction of buying, not out of need. I never saw this buying habit as a selfish desire.

After the verse in 2 Peter informed me that I was to *learn* to put aside my selfish desires, its teaching even went with me into that clothing store. With this Scripture verse in mind, I experienced God's help as I exercised the third step of the game plan. I went into that store one day, looked carefully through each clothing rack, and found that nothing appealed to me. I walked out of the store without a package.

To affirm what had happened, I went back the next day to make sure I hadn't missed any of the racks. Same result. I went out empty-handed.

As I got to know God better, he helped me put aside some of my selfish desires for clothing. I still enjoy attractive clothes, but I'm learning to discern between what I want and what I need. God keeps teaching me to use moderation in spending, and when I listen, my degree of wanting drops drastically.

Not everything you do for yourself should be considered a selfish desire, but as you keep this step in mind, God will help you know when a desire *becomes* selfish.

The purpose of this third step is to teach you to "become patient and godly, gladly letting God have his way with you" (2 Pet. 1:6b).

Game Plan: Step Four. You'd think the game plan would end with allowing God to have his way in your life, but it doesn't! Verse 7 completes the plan.

This final step makes it possible for you to *"enjoy* other people . . . *like* them, and finally you will grow to *love* them deeply." We all have contacts with many kinds of people. A number of those contacts are extremely satisfying. Our lives are enriched because of these different personalities. We enjoy being with them. But we also have met and worked with others who have rubbed us the wrong way, whose opinions and goals are different from ours.

Perhaps we have met extremists who either think they don't know or can't do anything, and some we have labeled "obnoxious" because they give the impression that they know and can do everything. We don't like these people. We don't enjoy being around them, and the last thing we have in mind is to love them.

When this fourth step is initiated in your life, I believe God can help you to like other people and even come to *enjoy* and *love* them. It's going to happen because God promised it would.

A Basic Command. After I discovered the practical guidelines in 2 Peter 1:3-8, I had no choice but to memorize the passage. I wanted to have instant recall of the steps so I could check myself out and see whether I was living by God's plans or trying to rearrange them. Since I had enough trouble memorizing zip codes and my Social Security number, I questioned whether I could memorize a passage of Scripture. But I did!

As I memorized this passage, I gained fresh appreciation for another Scripture passage: "And these words, which I am commanding you today, shall be on your heart . . . and you shall bind them as a sign on your hand and they shall be as frontals on your forehead. And you shall write them on the doorposts of your house and on your gates" (Deut. 6:6, 8, 9, NASB).

It had been a long time since I had tried to memorize any Scripture. The challenge must have worn off when I stopped getting gold stars in Sunday school for Scripture memorization. But God's command has always been to hide his words in our hearts—not just in our memories where we tend to forget, but in our hearts where even memory can't take them from us.

"But, God, you've seen how I reacted in fear when my teachers gave assignments to memorize. You heard me stumble through Lincoln's Gettysburg Address and the Preamble to the Constitution. You saw how my cold hands shook as I sat in front of a group of restless parents and struggled to remember notes I had tried to memorize for my piano recitals."

I primed myself with every known excuse not to memorize the Scriptures, but God canceled all of them. He reminded me that "I can do everything God asks me to with the help of Christ who gives me the strength and power" (Phil. 4:13). His Word was to be so firmly embedded in my heart that I could say about each Scripture verse I memorized, "Now I've got it. It's mine!"

Instead of memorizing a certain amount of Scripture each week, as some plans suggest, I follow a much more flexible plan which requires no certain amount.

Before you choose a Scripture passage to memorize, ask God to lead you to a verse or a section that relates directly to you. If you're more comfortable starting with shorter verses, fine. God teaches some powerful lessons in some of the shorter verses.

If you memorize longer verses or passages, start

with the first phrase, and the following day memorize the next phrase. Repeat your new phrase along with the phrase you learned the day before. Keep adding to and repeating each phrase until you don't have to peek at the verses. Stay with them until they roll out of your mouth automatically, like the multiplication tables. Write them down. Say them three times a day for a week, even two weeks, and I assure you by then they will be yours.

God had a purpose for commanding us to hide his words in our hearts. He knew we would experience tense, frightening, and heartbreaking circumstances and that these hidden words would help us through those times.

The result of seeking out and hiding God's Word in our hearts is found at the end of Psalm 119:11: "they [will] hold me back from sin."

The three basics outlined in the second special truth are these: (1) learn some basic Christian concepts; (2) follow the rules set up in God's basic game plan; (3) submit to his basic command to memorize his Word. These basics exemplify the practicality of God's Word.

🌺 Confronting Yourself

I. What one new fact have you gained from this chapter? Record and share it.

_____

II. Suppose:
   A. You have no cooking utensils. What basic items will you buy?
   1.

   2.

   3.

   4.

   B. You are to purchase four basic items for a new baby. What will you buy?
   1.

   2.

   3.

   4.

C. You have no cosmetics. What four basic items will you buy?

1.

2.

3.

4.

D. You know nothing about God. What basic(s) will you need to learn about him?

_____

III. Search out the basic concepts from the Scripture verses below. Which ones teach:

A. You are to praise and glorify God.

1.

2.

B. You are to please God.

1.

2.

C. You are to grow continually in your relationship with God.

1.

2.

1 Thessalonians 4:11   2 Peter 3:18
Colossians 1:10b   Psalm 106:2
Revelation 4:11   Hebrews 11:6a

Share what you believe to be another basic
Christian concept. What Scripture passages support
your belief?

IV. In chapter 2, consider the steps under "A Basic
Game Plan." Confront yourself. "Have I overlooked
one of the steps? If so, which one?" Answer: "What
can I do to get the steps in order?"

V. God has many plans that branch out from his
Master Plan. Look at the following plans and find
the results that will be produced when the plans are
carried out. (Study from at least two versions of the
Bible.)

GOD'S PLAN   *RESULTS OF THE PLAN*

A. Wait on me
                                        Isaiah 40:31, KJV

B. How to live
                                        1 Thessalonians 4:11,
                                        12, TLB

C. Admit your sins
                                        Psalm 32:5, NIV, TLB

D. Obey my voice
_____
Jeremiah 7:23, KJV

E. Let the Holy Spirit
control your life
_____
Galatians 5:22, 23, KJV

F. Put on my armor
_____
Ephesians 6:11, KJV

Which plan do you need to incorporate more fully into your life?

_____

VI. Many verses have been discussed. Which one most closely relates to you now? Live with that verse this week. Memorize it. After you have "hidden it in your heart," make a phone call to someone in your group and repeat the verse.

_____

VII. Write a prayer of thanks that conveys a new truth you have learned from this study/discussion. Pray the prayer with one other person.

_____

VIII. Make a resolution that will help meet an immediate need in your life.
RESOLVE:

STRETCHING
EXERCISES

Open my eyes to see wonderful things in
your Word.

FIRST DAY:
"Now all praise to God for his wonderful kindness to us
and his favor that he has poured out upon us, because
we belong to his dearly loved Son" (Eph. 1:6).

SECOND DAY:
"I want you to trust me in your times of trouble, so I can
rescue you, and you can give me glory" (Ps. 50:15).

THIRD DAY:
"You can never please God without faith, without
depending on him" (Heb. 11:6a).

FOURTH DAY:
"When a man's ways are pleasing to the Lord, he makes
even his enemies to be at peace with him" (Prov. 16:7,
NASB).

FIFTH DAY:
"But O my soul, don't be discouraged. Don't be upset.
Expect God to act! For I know that I shall again have
plenty of reason to praise him for all that he will do. He
is my help! He is my God!" (Ps. 42:11).

SIXTH DAY:
"But grow in grace (undeserved favor, spiritual strength) and recognition and knowledge and understanding of our Lord and Savior Jesus Christ, the Messiah. To Him (be) glory (honor, majesty and splendor) both now and to the day of eternity . . ." (2 Pet. 3:18, Amp.).

SEVENTH DAY:
"For the reverence and fear of God are basic to all wisdom. Knowing God results in every other kind of understanding" (Prov. 9:10).

ADVANCED STRETCHING EXERCISE
"For everything comes from God alone. Everything lives by his power, and everything is for his glory. To him be glory evermore" (Rom. 11:36).

3
When a Woman Listens to God

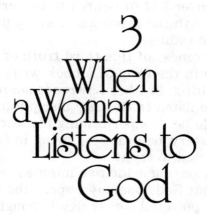

If you're like most women, you're too busy! You might be busy developing your career, maintaining a good marriage, being a good parent. You probably work faithfully in your church, make sure you don't neglect people with special needs, and keep your house presentable in case someone comes by unexpectedly. Like the proverbial "Martha," you're so busy that you find it next to impossible to take time to listen to your husband, children, and friends, much less to God. It isn't that you don't *want* to listen to God, but all your interests and demands pull you away from him instead of drawing you closer to him.

Somewhere within the development of your spiritual life it becomes crucial to get involved in the third special truth of listening to God. Listening to him can help you balance your career with the rest of the demands on your time. It can strengthen your marriage. Your relationship with your children can improve. You can learn where God wants you to serve in your church. Also, you will no longer feel pressured to be personally involved with the problems of every person within a 500-mile radius.

My awareness of this third truth of listening to God came in the form of a book written by a monk. In his writing, Brother Lawrence shared how he learned to listen to God. By disciplining his mind, even while he was performing his kitchen duties in the monastery, he practiced being in God's presence and I wanted to try it.

I began setting aside two minutes each day to think about God. One day I spent the time thinking about his power. Another day I thought about his love. On other days I'd think about his forgiveness or his knowledge. At times I read Scripture passages that specifically revealed the attributes of God. As I practiced being in his presence through the Scriptures, I learned that he would work out his plans for my life (Ps. 138:8) and strengthen and help me (Isa. 40:29). I discovered that I wouldn't escape troubles, but God would help me with them (Ps. 34:19). He kept saying that he was with me wherever I went (Josh. 1:9). In that two-minute recess each day I learned to wait on God. Psalm 27:14 says, "*Wait* for the Lord. . . . Yes, wait and he will help you." The use of the word "wait" in this verse goes beyond sitting and waiting for God to do something. The psalmist says to "anticipate," "be full of hope," "*wait until* you expect God to act!"

This kind of waiting is in total opposition to the fast pace you and I keep. It bothers us when we have to wait on *anything*. We don't have time to enjoy the aroma of a potato baking in a regular oven for an hour when we know it can be microwaved in five minutes. That domestic detail may not be a major concern, but it's one small fact stacked up against hundreds of others similar to it, and each one reminds us that we don't have time to

wait. Until we consent to the idea of waiting for
God, we continue to experience high levels of
frustration, anger, tension, and other stress
symptoms.

There's a gradual progression involved in waiting
on God. When a woman waits on God to the extent
of expecting him to act, she begins to "listen" (Rom.
10:17). When she *listens* to God, her strength is
"renewed" (Isa. 40:31). When she's *renewed* she's
ready for God to "help" her (Ps. 121:2). The
progression results in her expecting to receive
whatever it is she needs in "God's way" (Ps. 37:34).

This is a magnificent, workable formula, but it
contradicts the part of your nature that makes you
want to do things *your way*. Because your way
works most of the time, your self-confidence
pours over into your spiritual life, and you
unintentionally tell God what you think is best.

You get your plans made and you set out to be
the best in your profession, have the best marriage,
be the best parent. Your plans look good on paper,
but they may not be what God has in mind. Since
God knows what is best for you, he sometimes
chooses to reconstruct your plans. It's during the
reconstruction period that you have the choice of
waiting and anticipating what God is going to do or
else of continuing to hang onto your stubborn way
of doing things.

As I practiced waiting on God, I discovered in
Scripture a tremendous example of waiting. The
Bible tells about Jesus' reaction when he got the
news that his friend Lazarus, in Judea, was very
sick. Even though Jesus loved Lazarus, "He stayed
where he was for the next two days and made no
move to go to [him]" (John 11:6). After two days,
Jesus said to his disciples, "Let's go to Judea"
(v. 7).

When I read that account, I wondered why Jesus

didn't go to be with Lazarus as soon as he heard
his friend was sick. I came to understand that it
pleased God for him to wait. Clearly, the events
that followed his arrival in Judea promoted "the
glory of God" (John 11:4).

The following Scripture verses and comments
reflect some of the practical lessons learned as I
have listened to God through his Word.

PRACTICAL LESSON ONE: PUT GOD FIRST
"But seek ye first the kingdom of God, and his
righteousness; and all these things shall be added
unto you" (Matt. 6:33, KJV).

Even though I have been familiar with this verse
for a long time, God taught me a different lesson
from it after all my children left home. I didn't
know how the "empty nest" would affect me. While
all the children were at home, the idea of sitting in
an empty nest sounded glorious! But when our last
daughter married and moved far away from home,
the nest no longer had as many positive qualities to
recommend it.

I did well the first week our daughter was gone
because my husband and I were on vacation that
same week. It was after I got home, went into her
room, and faced her empty closet that I realized
that my responsibilities as a full-time mother—a
nonstop span of twenty-nine years—were over. I
felt terribly lonely and misplaced. Tears came for
the first time since our daughter's wedding. During
the next several days, I cried at regular and
irregular intervals, in convenient and inconvenient
locations.

Every time I saw my daughter's favorite cereal
while I was grocery shopping, I'd cry. When I drove
past the doughnut shop where she and I had talked

about school and her engagement and wedding
plans, I'd start to cry again. As I heard songs that
she had sung, the results were the same. I kept
reading the Scriptures faithfully for reassurance—
but the loneliness persisted. I finally admitted to
God that I needed help.

I gained some perspective by reading a Christian
magazine article written by a missionary who had
been separated from her children at the outbreak
of World War II. During the separation she had no
way of knowing how the enemy was treating her
children. In her anxiety she prayed that God would
keep them safe. She remembered that years before
a friend had shared with her his interpretation of
Matthew 6:33: "When you take care of the things
that are dear to God, he will take care of the
things that are dear to you." She started
immediately ministering to the people of China
who were dear to God, and she believed God would
take care of her children. Five years later her
family was reunited. Miraculously, the children had
not been mistreated by the enemy.

After I finished reading the article, I knew what
I had to do. I would remain faithful in the things
that were dear to God and trust him to take over
the care of my children. Once more I released my
daughters back to God. I thanked him for giving to
each one a husband who loved her. I prayed that
those young women would become as dear to their
husbands as they were to me. I started a new life
that day, minus children running through the house
or teens coming in late at night.

I believe God when he says that he wants us to
enjoy our children; but I also believe our children
are never to become more important to us than he
is. He wants us to enjoy other things, such as our
houses; but we aren't to take so much interest in

them that we neglect our relationship with him. He
wants us to have proper clothing; but clothing is
never to become more important than he is. He
wants us to enjoy eating; but neither is food to
take precedence over him. God promises that when
we follow the first part of this verse, "eager to
have God as your king" (Matt. 6:33, Beck),
whatever else we *need*, he'll provide.

PRACTICAL LESSON TWO: SET PERSONAL PRIORITIES

"This should be your ambition: to live a quiet life,
minding your own business and doing your own
work" (1 Thess. 4:11).

Here is an "all things done in moderation," three-
step guide for a satisfying and productive life.

When you hear God saying, "live a quiet life,"
he's telling you to *practice* being quiet. (Nothing
pleases Satan more than to get you disquieted.)
Next, God says to "mind your own business."
Matthew Henry's One-Volume Commentary has a
frank interpretation of this phrase. "Those who are
busybodies, meddling in other men's matters
generally have but little quiet in their own minds
and cause great disturbances among their
neighbors, at least they seldom mind . . . to be
diligent in their own calling." Finally, God tells you
to "do your own work." You are to concentrate on
what *he* wants you to do and not take up your time
thinking about or telling others how they should do
their work.

This verse set off a chain reaction that helped me
get rid of some unnecessary activities. I became
aware that other people's business was to become
my business only when they confided in me and
asked me to help or to pray for them. This allowed

me time to set attainable goals with definite purposes and to stick with them.

Reading 1 Thessalonians 4:11 shrunk my work to a manageable size. It was a relief to know that it wasn't and never would be my business to shape the whole world's present or future needs. I was only to help with the needs nearest me. This also gave me time to take better care of myself.

Whenever you are tempted to disregard 1 Thessalonians 4:11, proceed immediately to verse 12 to hear God say, "As a result [of following this three-step guide], people who are not Christians will trust and respect you."

PRACTICAL LESSON THREE: USE THE RIGHT MOTIVES

"We can justify our every deed but God looks at our motives" (Prov. 21:2).

> If a man comes into your church dressed in expensive clothes and with valuable gold rings on his fingers, and at the same moment another man comes in who is poor and dressed in threadbare clothes, and you make a lot of fuss over the rich man and give him the best seat in the house and say to the poor man: "You can stand over there if you like, or else sit on the floor"—well, judging a man by his wealth shows that you are guided by *wrong motives* (James 2:2-4).

Can you imagine how applying these verses for a week might change what you do? Before you did *anything,* you'd probably stop and ask, "What motive do I have for doing this?" You face daily situations that lend themselves to that question.

Why do you invite guests into your home for a meal? Is it so they will return your invitation or simply because you want to be hospitable?

Why do you dress your children the way you do? Is it so they won't be the only ones without a certain designer label on their pockets or so that they'll be dressed comfortably and adequately?

Why do you prepare the kinds of meals you do? Is it so you might break the present record set for fast-food service, because you need a compliment, or because you want to provide nutritious meals for your family and insure their good health?

Why do you accept certain responsibilities within your church? For recognition, to make yourself a likely candidate for the next Christian saint, or because you know you're doing what you believe God wants you to do?

A wrong motive is doing anything in order to impress others and draw attention to yourself. A right motive pleases and honors God.

As you listen to God speak through this verse from Proverbs, it should help reduce the pharisaical tendency to covet approval from others instead of from God.

PRACTICAL LESSON FOUR:
PRAY ABOUT PROBLEMS
It would be difficult to estimate how many books have been written to help people solve their problems. Some may be helpful, but God has always had a plan available for solving problems for those who would listen to him. This plan is evident in Psalm 3:1-6.

King David's problem was that his son, as well as others, were planning to kill him. "So many seek to harm me. I have so many enemies. So many say that God will never help me" (vv. 1, 2).

David did what few people are able to do; he turned away from his problem even though it hadn't been solved, and he turned his complete attention toward God. He laid out his problem and then prayed, "But Lord, you are my shield, my glory, and my only hope. You alone can lift my head. . . . I cried out to the Lord, and he heard me from his Temple in Jerusalem" (vv. 3, 4).

The result of David's prayer showed me what happens when God is included in problem solving. After David prayed, he wrote, "I lay down and slept in peace and woke up safely, for the Lord was watching over me. And now, *although* ten thousand enemies surround me on every side, *I am not afraid*" (v. 5).

More often than we might admit, we reverse this procedure. We try one or more of our five problem-solving techniques before we include God in our problems. We try such techniques as: (1) Constantly thinking about the problem. This particular method frustrates us. (2) Talking to our husbands and friends. Talking helps, but it may not completely solve the problem. (3) Staying busy so we don't have time to think about the problem. The flaw in this method is that sooner or later our energy is depleted and we have to stop. When we stop, we find the problem is still there. (4) Pretending the problem doesn't exist. Facing the problem may be too painful. (5) Worrying. This compounds the problem.

God teaches that *before* we try to solve our own problems we are to lay them out completely before him, believing that he knows and cares and will help us solve them. Each time our thoughts turn to our problems we're to take them to God. He will either help us solve them, or through his grace he

will miraculously enable us to accept our situation
and cope with it.

After studying Psalm 3, I reevaluated my past
problem-solving techniques. They didn't work! I
had worried for hours and had spent sleepless
nights without finding solutions. I still try to
handle my problems—but not by myself, since
I have learned that God waits and wants to
be "my hiding place from *every* storm of life"
(Ps. 32:7).

PRACTICAL LESSON FIVE:
DON'T BE AFRAID

"What time I am afraid, I will trust in thee" (Ps.
56:3, KJV).

The first time I thought much about this verse
was when I introduced it to our youngest daughter
after she admitted she was afraid of the dark. I
encouraged her to quote the verse every time she
became afraid. It helped her, but it also reminded
me that everyone has certain fears.

Many women's fears are grouped into two general
categories: family and health. Some mothers fear
that they might follow the wrong principles with
their children and ruin their lives. They are afraid
that their children might get the wrong schoolteachers and that the teachers will ruin the
children if the mothers don't.

Mothers are afraid that if their children don't
start wearing a scarf or cap by the end of
September and keep it on until spring, or if they
get uncovered at night while they're asleep, or if
they sit and watch a football game in subzero
temperatures, they'll develop pneumonia.

Mothers are afraid their teens might make

mistakes that will permanently alter the direction of their lives.

Is there a woman alive who hasn't had a persistent headache and feared that she had a brain tumor? A pain in her chest (probably due to having at least one toddler or teenager living with her) is surely a heart attack. Through the news media she hears that everything from tinting her graying hair to eating bacon causes cancer.

Many women fear their husbands may die before they do and life will become stagnant and unbearably lonely. That particular fear invaded my life late one evening.

My husband woke me and told me he was having severe abdominal cramps. I had never seen him in such pain. I called the doctor, described the symptoms, and he instructed me to take my husband to the hospital emergency room. Between the time I called the doctor and our arrival at the hospital—a span of ten minutes—I not only envisioned an operation for my husband, but the thought of his death also crossed my mind. Upon arrival at the hospital, his pain subsided and two pills solved his problem.

At the height of my fear, I silently repeated over and over, "What time I am afraid, I *will* trust in thee." I *was* afraid. I had every reason to fear, and yet I was also able to include God in my fear by repeating his promise to me.

A BY-PRODUCT OF LISTENING

I have always enjoyed reading the story of the little boy who shared his lunch with Jesus and how Jesus fed more than five thousand with it. The main thrust of the story has always been the miracle, but now I recognize an additional truth. The reason *why* this child didn't hesitate to share his lunch must have been because he had spent the morning listening to Jesus. Because he had listened he was ready, not only to see a miracle, but also to become a part of it.

The difference between seeing miracles happen and being a part of those miracles may be the application of the special truth of *listening to God.*

🌺 Confronting Yourself

I. Write in one sentence something new that you learned in this chapter.

II. A Hearing Test:
Sit by the person you know least. Listen as she tells you some facts about herself. Do not write down the facts. (Time limit: two minutes.)
A. full name
B. shoe size
C. way she likes her eggs prepared
D. a funny/happy childhood memory
E. something that makes her angry
F. person she admires

Without being prompted (or using notes), share these facts with the group. If you had to be prompted it may indicate that you need to listen more closely.

III. How well do you *wait?*
Write "P" by the situations you have problems handling. Write "NP" by the situations you have no problems handling.
_____A. dinner guests arriving thirty minutes late

___B. still sitting in a doctor's office at 3:00 for a 2:00 appointment

___C. standing in a checkout line behind a person who obviously grocery shops monthly

___D. waiting for a traffic light to turn green

___E. trying to start a car on a cold morning

___F. receiving a notice: "The item ordered is temporarily out of stock. Reorder"

___G. locking keys in the car when you're already late for an appointment

Tell the person closest to you which situation gives you the most problems. The least problems.

If you wrote "P" by five or more situations, ask God to slow you down to enable you to wait more patiently, especially on him.

IV. Read each of these verses from two Bible translations, and in ten words or less write what you hear in:

A. Ecclesiastes 3:7b

B. Psalm 27:14

C. Proverbs 3:6

D. 1 Peter 5:7

E. Psalm 32:7, 8

Which verse is most relevant to you? Share the
verse and what you wrote. Ask if anyone else heard
what you heard in the verse.

V. To get a firm grasp of the following Scripture
passage, answer these questions after reading
Colossians 2:2-11. Use as many Bible translations
as necessary to pull out the truths.

A. The main lesson is:

B. The best verse is:

C. What do these verses tell you either about God,
Jesus, or the Holy Spirit?

D. Is there an example for you to follow?

E. Are you being commanded to do anything?

F. What promise is there for you to claim?

G. What verse could change your life?

VI. Form a circle by joining hands. In silence, each woman should "practice the presence of God" for two minutes as suggested in this chapter.

After this time, someone can begin a sentence prayer of praise. Continue until everyone has raised her voice in praise.

Sing: "Praise God from Whom All Blessings Flow."

VII. This week, read and study the outline from Psalm 3:1-6 for solving a problem. Lay out the problem before God. Be specific (family, job, a relationship, conflict, etc.). At the end of the week, share with a friend how you've had victory over the problem or how God is helping you cope with it.

VIII. Write a resolution concerning your desire to listen to God more closely through his Word.
   RESOLVE:

S T R E T C H I N G
E X E R C I S E S

Open my eyes to see wonderful things in
your Word.

FIRST DAY:
"The wise man learns by listening" (Prov. 21:11a).

SECOND DAY:
"For since the world began no one has seen or heard of
such a God as ours, who works for those who wait for
him!" (Isa. 64:4).

THIRD DAY:
"In everything you do, put God first, and he will direct
you and crown your efforts with success" (Prov. 3:6).

FOURTH DAY:
"The Lord is wonderfully good to those who wait for him,
to those who seek for him. It is good both to hope and
wait quietly for the salvation of the Lord" (Lam. 3:25,
26).

FIFTH DAY:
"The Lord is good. When trouble comes, he is the place
to go!" (Nah. 1:7a).

SIXTH DAY:
"Morning by morning he wakens me and opens my
understanding to his will. The Lord God has spoken to
me and I have listened" (Isa. 50:4b, 5).

SEVENTH DAY:
"Let him have all your worries and cares, for he is always thinking about you and watching everything that concerns you" (1 Pet. 5:7).

ADVANCED STRETCHING EXERCISE
"Faith comes from listening . . ." (Rom. 10:17).

4
Accepting God's Kind of Forgiveness

If you were going to have a recurring problem with any one of the special truths in this book, your problem probably would be with the fourth truth: accepting God's kind of forgiveness. You might be quick to ask God to forgive your sins but then continue to live with unnecessary guilt feelings.

God's truth about forgiveness is found throughout the Scriptures. It's as though he's saying, "Don't overlook this truth. It can liberate you from feelings of guilt. You *must* learn what I'm teaching about forgiveness."

God knows you're imperfect; therefore, he has set up a *perfect* solution to eliminate the sins that "come so readily" upon you (Heb. 12:1, Bas.). The solution involves recognizing your sins, confessing them, and accepting God's kind of forgiveness.

RECOGNIZING SINS
God clearly explains in his Word what pleases him, but he also helps you recognize what things

displease him, by listing many sins. In Proverbs
6:16-19 he plainly states what he hates; and what
God hates, you must exclude from your life. The
writer of Proverbs says that God hates for people
to "devise wicked plans" (v. 18, NASB), to be
"[eager] to do wrong" (v. 19). He hates for people to
hurt others deliberately by telling lies about them,
spreading strife.

Years ago I was part of a neighborhood group
which met weekly for a social time. Even before
our first cups of coffee were emptied, many of our
conversations had started with "Did you hear about
. . . ?" "I can't believe she would . . ." and "Is it true
that . . . ?"

I myself asked some of those questions. I also
answered some of them even when I didn't have
full knowledge of what was being asked. Other
times I wouldn't say anything. I didn't have to. By
shrugging my shoulders, raising my eyebrows,
rolling my eyes slowly, or shaking my head from
side to side I indicated that I agreed with what
was being said. I voluntarily allowed myself to
become a part of the things God said he hated. It
wasn't until I recognized what I was doing as sin,
that I could admit it to God and then walk away
from that weekly gathering.

There are many other sins that displease God. It
displeases him when his children worry (Phil. 4:6),
allow jealousy or envy to be nurtured (Exod.
20:17), feed their habit of fear (Ps. 56:3), or justify
their bad tempers and impatience (1 Cor. 13:4). It
displeases him when his children don't take time to
nourish their beautiful, complex bodies (1 Cor.
6:20). He hates for them to fall into the trap of
speaking thoughtlessly and condemningly to their
family members, and stubbornly refusing to forgive
someone who has wronged them (Matt. 18:21, 22).

Negligence displeases God (James 4:17)—neglecting to make a phone call ("Lord, you *are* aware of how busy I am, aren't you?"), to write a note ("I meant to"), or to invite people for a meal ("I would if my house were larger!").

God has provided a perfect plan to help you recognize sins. He gives you the Holy Spirit, whose job it is to penetrate the depths of your soul and expose you for what you are, a person who has sinned and needs to be cleansed.

CONFESSING SINS

When you recognize your sin, the next step is an honest, verbal admission to God that you have sinned. This step allows the healing to begin. You may recognize your sin and still hesitate to confess it even though God says to confess your sin as soon as you are aware of it (Ps. 32:6).

This hesitancy may go back to your childhood when you were confronted by your parents after you had done wrong. When you were small you didn't hesitate to admit what you had done. "Yes, I cut pieces out of the curtain with my brand new scissors." "*I* was the one who colored my baby doll with your lipstick and laid it on the white bedspread." "I picked the bouquet out of the neighbor's yard." Those honest admissions may have brought such painful results that, as you got older, you tried to hide what you had done or lie in order to avoid the consequences.

While I was single and living at home with my parents, I remember washing dishes one evening and letting a plate slip from my hands. When I picked it up, I noticed a tiny piece of its edge had chipped off. I quickly dried the plate and placed it at the bottom of the stack of plates in the cabinet,

making sure the chipped part was out of view—
especially out of my mother's view. I didn't have
the courage to tell her what had happened.

It has been a long time since that incident. I
never did tell Mother about it. I had no way of
knowing what her reaction might have been; I only
know I was afraid to admit to her what I had done.
I also remember that I didn't want her to be
unhappy with me. I have no doubt now that she
would have understood and told me it was all right.
Admitting what I had done would have been such a
simple solution, but I couldn't tell her.

Experiences similar to this may stay in your
memory, causing you to be more hesitant to admit
your sins to God. You aren't sure how he'll respond
to your confessions, so you keep stacking "chipped
plates," trying to conceal mistakes from God as
though he won't know if you don't tell him.

You may have gotten into the habit of ignoring or
justifying some of your sins; or perhaps you fear
you've committed a sin so damaging that even if
you confessed it, God could never forgive it.

Another reason you might hesitate to confess
your sins is that you can't win over your stubborn
will. While I was writing this book, there was a sin
I needed to confess, but my stubbornness kept me
from doing it. The sin involved a woman who had
accused me of something I hadn't done. It was easy
to ignore the sin because I seldom saw the woman.
When I did see her, I pretended I didn't so I
wouldn't have to speak to her. Yet avoiding her
didn't alleviate the uneasy feeling I had in my
stomach every time I saw her.

I talked with my husband about the problem. I
confessed my sin to God, but something was still
wrong. I needed to confess my wrong to the
woman. As soon as the force of that truth struck
me, I phoned her to ask if I could come to her

house. She agreed. It took me approximately thirty minutes to bring up the subject of our disagreement. When I did, both of us realized that the bad feelings between us had come from a series of misunderstandings. Neither of us talked in condemning tones. We were ready to make things right between us.

After our time together, I was liberated from that sin. I had taken the necessary steps toward receiving God's kind of forgiveness. I had lost so many valuable hours by hanging onto my stubborn will and ignoring God's command about confessing sins.

God doesn't want you to hesitate to confess or to try to hide your sins. He waits for you to confess them. He knows how much better you will feel after you do. He *encourages* you to confess. "No matter how deep your stain is or how awful it may be, I can remove it and make you as clean as freshly fallen snow. Even if your stain is as red as crimson, even if you've been soaking in it, I can take it out of your life" (paraphrased from Isa. 1:18-20).

After you confess your sin to God, the next step is to learn *how* God forgives you.

ACCEPTING GOD'S FORGIVENESS

God has a perfect way to remove sins from your life. When you confess to him, he "blots away your sins . . . and will never think of them again" (Isa. 43:25).

If you're twenty-five years old or less, you may find it difficult to believe that there haven't always been ballpoint pens. Before the ballpoint pen was invented, fountain pens were used. These pens had hollow tubes inside them which were filled with liquid ink. At times, while the pen was in use, a blob of ink might come out of the pen onto the paper. The writer would use an ink blotter to absorb the excess ink off the paper. Still, there would be a trace of ink remaining on the paper. This is the way most of us forgive. With our mouths we say, "I forgive you," but there's still a trace of an unforgiving spirit. With God it is different. God says that after we are aware of our sins and confess them to him, they are "wiped out" (Acts 3:19a, Gspd.).

Satan wants to keep you from accepting God's kind of forgiveness. He keeps a twenty-four-hour vigil, trying to conceal God's complete forgiveness. If he can't stop your confession, he listens closely as you obey the first two steps; then he tries to sidetrack you before you accept God's complete forgiveness. Satan doesn't want you to hear God's voice saying, "It's all right now. You've done what I've commanded you to do."

It's imperative that you hear the whole truth about God's forgiveness. Psalm 32:3-5 outlines the three steps that bring that kind of forgiveness.

RECOGNIZE YOUR SIN: "There was a time when I wouldn't admit what a sinner I was. But my dishonesty made me miserable and filled my days with frustration. All day and all night your hand was heavy on me. My strength evaporated like water on a sunny day . . ." (vv. 3, 4).

CONFESS YOUR SIN: "I finally admitted all my sins to you and stopped trying to hide them. I said to myself, 'I will confess them to the Lord' " (v. 5a).

ACCEPT GOD'S FORGIVENESS: "And you forgave me! *All* my guilt is gone" (v. 5b).

RECOGNIZE CRITICISM AS SIN
There are many sins waiting to assault your life, but there is one sin that's more prone to attack a

woman than almost any other sin. It's the sin of criticism. One good reason for this may be because she practices it diligently, daily. Perhaps it's such an integral part of her thoughts and speech that she doesn't even recognize it as sin. Where does criticism start? It can be produced by conflicts of personalities, goals, or opinion. "People don't do things the way *I* would do them." A woman can justify criticism by adding another word to it. Suddenly it becomes "constructive" criticism. This cover-up prolongs her refusal to recognize criticism as sin.

If you don't admit that criticism is sin, soon it will affect your whole family. When your husband didn't change the way you expected him to change the hour after your wedding ceremony, did you criticize him? Do you squeeze criticism into the lives of your children when they don't measure up to your expectations or do things the way you would do them? When your home gets too small to hold your habit of criticism, do you go outside your home and criticize friends, brief acquaintances, and total strangers?

Have you ever sat in restaurants, churches, and other public places observing the people, and thought, "Can you believe that outfit?" "How did *she* get him?" "You'd think they could have more control over their children." "I've never seen a healthier set of hips!" Such sly remarks and tongue-in-cheek humor keep rolling out of your unguarded mouth, and criticism eventually takes over your conversation. It becomes easy to criticize your employer, schoolteachers, minister, and certainly politicians because they seldom measure up to your expectations or agree with your opinions.

Since criticism doesn't edify a person or please

God, it must be recognized as sin. When God says, "Don't criticize," and you do, it's sin. With the sharp clarity of God's command, recognizing criticism as sin is not a choice, it's mandatory.

CONFESSING A CRITICAL SPIRIT

Catherine Marshall once wrote about how God impressed her to recognize the sin of her critical spirit. One morning she asked God to give her an assignment for that day. The assignment was discovered in Romans 14:13: "So don't criticize each other any more." She admitted that since she was inclined to be a perfectionist, she had a tendency to be highly critical not only of others, but also of herself. She admitted to God that she had a critical spirit and for one day she experimented with "fasting"—not from food, but from faultfinding. She determined to accept people as they were and to stop judging them.

Through the experiment she discovered that her critical spirit had stifled many creative ideas that perhaps God had wanted to give to her. It also prevented an expression of love to a person whose life had become sidetracked. Her critical spirit had also hurt a family relationship. What happened after she recognized and confessed her critical spirit was proof that a change was in progress—an indication that true confession had been made.

Ideas began to flow in a way she had not experienced for months. She wrote a letter to the young man expressing her love and she asked her child to forgive the anger she had directed toward him. She was able to release him from her opinion in a decision he was trying to make. God made it clear that she was not to try to manipulate him.

As I thought about Mrs. Marshall's experiment, I

became painfully aware of my own critical spirit. That awareness gave the Holy Spirit room to flood my memory with old sins which, until then, I had not even recognized as being sins.

As I confessed my critical spirit, I discovered that God was capable of changing other people without my telling him how to do it. Not once do I recall him ever calling on me as a character reference before he made the final decision about how to produce necessary changes in other people's lives.

I know I'm making progress because I'm no longer as comfortable when I criticize as I once was. When I do bow to my old critical spirit, I'm learning to confess that sin so the habit won't regain a hold on me.

THE RESULTS OF CONFESSING A CRITICAL SPIRIT

Until you recognize criticism as sin, you continue to be a participant in a game someone has called "stone-throwing." This game is played by those who believe they are without fault. They are so busy trying to take the speck from someone else's eye that they fail to see the log jam in their own eye. Because they picture themselves as "judges," they pick up their well-chosen stones and throw them at people who make them angry, or those with whom they disagree, or perhaps people who have disillusioned, hurt, or disappointed them. Until they allow God to renew his Spirit within them, they continue to play the game, hurting not only others but themselves and God as well.

Catherine Marshall summed up what she learned after she became aware that she was a "stone-thrower":

1. Whatever we see wrong in another, rather than criticizing him directly, or talking to someone else about it, try praying about it. Ask the Spirit of God to do the correcting Himself directly with the individual.
2. A carping, judgmental spirit focuses us in on ourselves and makes us unhappy, even has an ill-effect on us physically. We lose perspective and humor.
3. Such a faultfinding spirit blocks the positive, creative thoughts God longs to give us in the direction of solutions to our problems.
4. A critical spirit can prevent good relationships between individuals and often produces retaliatory criticism, as Jesus warns in Matthew 7:1-5.
5. Criticism blocks all the positive attributes of the Spirit of God—love, good will, mercy, understanding.

This Scripture seems to wrap it up for me: "So do not criticize at all; the hour of reckoning has still to come, when the Lord will come to bring dark secrets to the light and to reveal life's inner aims and motives. Then each of us will get his meed of praise from God" (1 Cor. 4:5, Mof.). (From *Guideposts* magazine, March 1983.)

After you have recognized and admitted the sin of a critical spirit, you still have two choices. You can either keep "throwing stones" at other people or you can choose to build altars to God with them. When you opt for the second choice, you can stand before your altar and thank God that the Holy Spirit has helped you recognize and overcome your critical spirit by confessing it and accepting his forgiveness.

After you confess any sin and accept God's kind of forgiveness, you can be free from unnecessary guilt feelings, and God can produce through your life a harvest of "love, joy, peace, patience, kindness, goodness, faithfulness" (Gal. 5:22). What a godly exchange for the fruits of the flesh.

🌸 Confronting Yourself

I. Is there a sin mentioned in this chapter that you had never recognized as a sin . . . until now? Have you confessed it? Have you accepted God's forgiveness?

II. Thinking of a person in a particular situation (past/present), how difficult is it to say "I'm sorry"? Write "D" for difficult; "ND" for not difficult.

___parent   ___friend

___husband   ___coworker

___child   ___neighbor

___child's teacher   ___God

Read Matthew 6:14, 15. How do the above categories you have marked "D" fit in with this teaching?

III. List the petitions David made to God during his
confession time in Psalm 51.

1.	11.
2.	12.
3.	13.
4.	14.
5.	15.
6.	16.
7.	17.
8.	18.
9.	19.
10.	20.

Compare your list with the rest of the group.
Have you prayed similar petitions? Which ones?

IV. Divide into two groups and read responsively:

When I confess my sins . . .
God "blots out and cancels your transgressions" and
"will not remember your sins" (Isa. 43:25,
Amp.).

When I confess my sins . . .
They are "wiped out" (Acts 3:19a, Gspd.).

When I confess my sins . . .
All my guilt is gone (Ps. 32:5b).

When I confess my sins . . .
They are gone like morning mist at noon (Isa.
44:22).

When I confess my sins . . .
The Lord will forgive and forget (Jer. 31:34).

When I confess my sins . . .
They are wiped out like a thick cloud (Isa. 44:22a,
NASB).

The more I confess my sins . . .
I see God's abounding grace forgiving me (Rom.
5:20).

Reverse the two groups and repeat.

Which word from God spoke most directly to you?
Memorize it and repeat it as you confess sins to God
to help you accept his kind of forgiveness.

V. Zacchaeus changed after he recognized and
confessed his sins. In Luke 19:1-8:
A. What is the subject?

B.   Who are the principle characters?

C. What evidence is there of genuine repentance in verse 8?

D. What example is there to follow?

VI. Offer up thanks for God's power to forgive and forget sins.

VII. *RESOLVE:* With God's help I will live out Romans 14:13.

Two days before your next meeting, omit one meal (if health permits). During that time, ask God to reveal any sin you may not have recognized and ask him to heal the memories of old sins that have been confessed.

Twenty-four hours before your next meeting, begin "fasting from faultfinding." Record and share the results. In which area did you find yourself to be most critical?

S T R E T C H I N G
E X E R C I S E S

Open my eyes to see wonderful things in
your Word.

FIRST DAY:
"Stop criticizing others, so that you may not be criticized
yourselves. For exactly as you criticize others, you will be
criticized" (Matt. 7:1, Wms.).

SECOND DAY:
"For lack of wood the fire goes out, and where there is
no whisperer, contention quiets down" (Prov. 26:20,
NASB).

THIRD DAY:
"I finally admitted all my sins to you and stopped trying
to hide them. I said to myself, 'I will confess them to the
Lord.' And you forgave me! All my guilt is gone" (Ps.
32:5).

FOURTH DAY:
"If we (freely) admit that we have sinned and confess
our sins, He is faithful and just (true to His own nature
and promises) and will forgive our sins (dismiss our
lawlessness) and continuously cleanse us from all
unrighteousness—everything not in conformity to His will
in purpose, thought and action" (1 John 1:9, Amp.).

FIFTH DAY:
"And having chosen us, he called us to come to him;
and when we came, he declared us 'not guilty,' filled us

with Christ's goodness, gave us right standing with himself, and promised us his glory" (Rom. 8:30).

SIXTH DAY:
"But if you sin, there is someone to plead for you before the Father. His name is Jesus Christ, the one who is all that is good and who pleases God completely. He is the one who took God's wrath against our sins upon himself, and brought us into fellowship with God; and he is the forgiveness for our sins, and not only ours but all the world's" (1 John 2:1b, 2).

SEVENTH DAY:
"I've blotted out your sins; they are gone like morning mist at noon! Oh, return to me, for I have paid the price to set you free" (Isa. 44:22).

ADVANCED STRETCHING EXERCISE
"So overflowing is his kindness toward us that he took away all our sins through the blood of his Son, by whom we are saved; and he has showered down upon us the richness of his grace . . ." (Eph. 1:7, 8a).

5
Accepting Your Body & Abilities

The fifth truth which you learn as you take God at his Word involves two very sensitive areas: accepting your body as God created it; and admitting that he has given you certain abilities to be discovered, developed, and used to bring honor to him.

Do you believe God is pleased with how he created you? To make sure you met his specifications, he was with your mother while you were being "knit together" in her womb. God saw you "before you were born and scheduled each day of your life *before* you began to breathe" (Ps. 139:16, author's paraphrase). God also gave you "the ability to do certain things well" (Rom. 12:6).

This truth affirms that you are a distinct part of God's Master Plan for the world. Consider the truth that you need to accept your body the way God made it.

Is it difficult for you to accept your own body? Have you hesitated to admit that God has given you special abilities for the purpose of bringing honor to him? If so, it's imperative that you include this fifth special truth in your life now. Otherwise, you might use large portions of your time criticizing your body and failing to recognize, develop, and use your abilities.

WHY IT'S DIFFICULT FOR A WOMAN TO ACCEPT HER BODY

I have suspected for several years that somewhere there is a group of people, probably all the same size, who meet together regularly and decide the standard for what is beautiful and acceptable. If you don't fall into any of their categories, you feel that you aren't acceptable. If you don't have straight teeth and good dental checkups, can't squeeze into a size ten of anything, aren't 5'7" tall, and don't weigh 120 pounds, their charts indicate that you aren't average.

These standards, interpreted by a woman who could never reach all of them at the same time, lead her to believe that she doesn't fit in anywhere. Women who already have a low self-image put great stock in these standards and can be damaged by them.

These unrealistic standards gave me problems for years. I still don't fully understand all that was involved in bringing me to accept my body the way God made it. It may have been a combination of my mental and spiritual maturing, or my determination to ignore the "law of averages." Whatever it was, I know that it became extremely important to acknowledge that I was of great value to God no matter how I looked.

During the early years of my marriage I discovered certain Scripture verses that helped me understand that I *was* valuable to God. "*God* has been made rich because we who are Christ's have been given to him!" (Eph. 1:18b). "For you love me so much!" (Ps. 86:13). "We have become gifts to God that he delights in . . ." (Eph. 1:11). "You have let me experience the joys of life and the exquisite pleasures of your own eternal presence" (Ps. 16:11). With these Scripture passages in mind, I admitted that I was of great value to God no matter how society's self-appointed Committee on Averages sized me up. The acceptance of my body played a strategic part in my discovering the potential that was within my body and in letting me become more useful to God.

HOW I LEARNED TO ACCEPT MY BODY

I don't ever recall asking my parents about it, but most of my life I had assumed that I was "born tall." I was approximately 5'10" by the time I was promoted to the eighth grade. I didn't realize that height would be a problem for me to accept. Then one day in school, as we all stood to say the Pledge of Allegiance to the Flag, I looked around and became acutely aware that I was taller than anyone else in the room. Nothing could have been more devastating to me. No one that age wants to be different from her peers in actions or appearance.

After I noticed that I was "different," I started to feel self-conscious and awkward. I was miserable at family reunions, especially as I listened to aunts and uncles make comments about my height. The more my family and friends tried, the less they were able to convince me that there would ever be any boys taller than I. To avoid my misery, I wanted to hide; but anyone as tall as I am doesn't hide well.

Through my high school years, the self-inflicted

wounds continued to build. It would be several years before I could thank God for my body, because I honestly believed he had gotten carried away when he created me.

Many times since then, I have thanked God for his continued grace during that adolescent period.

Many of my problems ended when I met the young man who was to become my husband. He was generous with his compliments. "You're beautiful." "You look great." I actually believed what he told me. With those regular affirmations he helped me to appreciate the positive aspects of my outward appearance.

I remember the life-changing day I specifically thanked God for my body—all of it. First, I thanked him for my height! Then I thanked him for the bump on the bridge of my nose, the dimple on my chin, the overlap of my two front teeth, and my freckles. I thanked him for my hair, skin, and eyes. I thanked him not only for the strong parts of my body but for the weak parts too. I became aware through his Word that, by refusing to accept myself, I had been rejecting what God had created.

Something unexpected happened after I accepted my body. I no longer criticized myself. I stopped comparing my outward appearance with other women's appearances. I stood straighter. It was clear that God's Word in 1 Corinthians 6:20 commanded me to glorify him in my body as well as my spirit, both of which were his. I changed my eating habits and began a daily exercise program.

Shortly after I accepted my body I made two resolutions: "I will show more respect to myself by taking better care of my body. And I will learn to camouflage the parts I can't change." I realized that my body would continue to change as I got older, and I learned to thank God for this.

Several years ago, I developed a skin disorder called vitaligo. This condition causes the colored pigment to leave the skin, making it prominently and permanently blotched. The final diagnosis was difficult to accept because I had always looked forward each summer to getting a deep tan. I was faced with the realization that I could not stay in the sun for long periods of time because my skin would burn easily. Because of this condition, I would no longer have what I considered to be beautiful skin. I eventually accepted this change in my body.

Next, I reached the menopause years. I had no way of knowing how this change would affect my body, but I learned quickly. From the first symptoms I kept thinking, "There has to be a better way!" Simultaneously with this change, the inevitable began to happen—outward hints of aging. Millions of other women experience this, but for some reason I never thought it would happen to me. I tried different ways to slow down the process, but after several unsuccessful attempts I realized that it defies postponement. Aging occurs on its own time schedule.

During that time I read the story of a woman about my age who had the courage to observe her body in front of a full-length mirror just after she stepped out of the shower. She commented that it looked as though everything on her had dropped a half inch. I couldn't have said it better!

Aging is inevitable, but a good attitude and a generous supply of acceptance and humor have much to do with how you continue to maintain your self-image.

God's Word helps a woman accept her body—the flaws, the parts she's self-conscious about, and the physical changes brought on by age. The Scriptures teach her that someday her body will be "incorruptible." There will no longer be reasons to consider having a facelift, getting dentures, being fitted with trifocals, wearing back braces or sturdy support hose. She will be fitted with a new body that will live forever (1 Cor. 15:52, 53).

HOW TO ACCEPT YOUR BODY

Do you ever wonder why you criticize your own body? Is it a habit? Do you feel you're expected to complain about certain parts of it—your hips, flat chest, weight? Evidently these topics are important to women, or how do you explain why they come up in the conversation whenever two or three women get together?

Tell yourself how you honestly feel about your appearance. Confront yourself. Do society's "averages" frustrate you? Are you so self-conscious about your appearance that it keeps you from performing to your greatest potential?

Give yourself a close examination in front of a full-length mirror. Instead of listing everything you don't like about yourself, concentrate on the parts you do like. Answer these questions: What part of your body do you have trouble accepting? Is there anything you can do about these trouble spots? If not, what's your choice? You aren't too tall, or too short. Your hair isn't too curly or too straight. So what if your skin is "terminally" white; you're knock-kneed; your ears, hands, or feet are larger than you think they need to be?

After you get yourself in plain view, instead of spending hours criticizing yourself, start searching the Scriptures and learn how valuable you are to God. Decide to commit your body to the One who created it and depend on him to use it.

PRESENT YOUR BODY TO GOD
If you've never prayed a prayer similar to this one,
pray it now.

> Lord, I've spent a lot of time criticizing
> myself, and I'm tired of doing it. Actually, I'm
> disgusted with myself. I've let a lot of
> opportunities get away because I have been
> so self-conscious about my appearance. I
> realize I'm contained within this body. There's
> no getting out of it. My wounds, many of
> them self-inflicted, are going to have to heal.
> Here I am, Lord. I have no idea what will be
> involved in this presentation, but take me the
> way I am right now.

I personally believe that a woman must make a
deliberate resolution to accept her body and
present it to God before she can be free of self-
rejection. She must tell her body every day, "I love
you," by the kind of food she puts into it, the
exercise she gives it, and the rest and relaxation
she allows for when she's tired.

Romans 12:1 (Amp.) stresses the significance of
the fifth special truth: "Make a decisive dedication
of your body—presenting all your members and
faculties—as a living sacrifice, holy (devoted,
consecrated) and well pleasing to God." This is a
necessary step if you are to experience firsthand
abundant living. It's surrendering yourself to God's
perfect will even though you don't know all that is
involved or what will be required of you. It's
allowing God to be in control of your whole person,
"spirit and soul and body" (1 Thess. 5:23).

Present your body to God the way it is. You don't
have to wait until you've dieted and lost ten
pounds or made any other alterations. God will let

you know later if you need to make some changes; but for now, present your body to him. This one vital presentation gives you a start toward being a more confident, joyful, satisfied woman of God.

WHY IT'S DIFFICULT TO ACCEPT YOUR ABILITIES

After you have accepted and presented your body to God, you can admit that he has given you some distinct abilities designed to bring glory to him. It isn't necessary that you make a formal declaration of your abilities, but it is vital that you announce them boldly to yourself.

There are women who excel in organizing meetings, daily schedules, weekly menus, and closets—as well as balancing their checkbook without a calculator. Others are good listeners or gracious hostesses. There are a few favored women who can make lovely floral arrangements. Some women are extremely sensitive to others' needs. They send cards, prepare meals for families going through stressful times, and know what to say to encourage others.

You are such a natural at what you do, you might not recognize these acts as special abilities given generously by God. You might have the tendency to skip over these "naturals" when you evaluate your abilities.

I rarely hear a woman admit that she has the ability to make a good pie crust. The reason she doesn't mention it is that she doesn't think it's important. The only ones who consider it important are women who are like I was, who *can't* make a first-class pie crust. When I mentioned to a group of women that it would mean a great deal to me to be able to make a good pie crust, one woman gave

me her "No-Fail Pie Crust" recipe. As she handed it
to me she said, "No one has ever failed with this
yet." A week later I used her recipe. Instant
success. I wrote to this young woman and
expressed my genuine appreciation for her
willingness to share something she does well.

What makes a woman downplay her abilities or
say at regular intervals, "I can't do anything"?
While reading a college professor's dissertation I
found an explanation for this universal statement
made by women. I learned that in the eighth
century men were actually afraid that if they spent
most of their time doing wrong, they would be
transformed into women at their reincarnation. It
was a long time—four hundred more years—before
a woman was thought to be good enough to eat
with her husband or was allowed to visit other
women.

Women's abilities stopped at the front door, as
they took care of their children, baked, washed,
and wove fabric for their families. One man
proudly admitted that he was committed to saying
three blessings each day, one being, "Thank you,
Lord, that you didn't make me a woman." He knew
what women were up against.

For years, the word "inferior" was aimed toward
women, and any recognition of their abilities
beyond their homes was slow in coming. Women's
restrictions slid on into the twentieth century and
continue to hold many back from using their God-
given abilities. Women constantly struggle with the
issue of self-worth.

At one Christian women's conference, a workshop
was offered on developing self-esteem. Practically
every woman who attended the conference made
sure she was registered for that workshop.

A guest lecturer on a college campus announced

that he would speak on the subject of accepting oneself. Before the meeting began, every seat was filled. Students were sitting in the aisles, lining the walls, and standing in the hall. It was evidence of the pervasive need for self-acceptance.

During a weekly Bible study, a group of women were asked to share an ability they felt they had. When one of the women started to respond, she paused for a moment and asked the group, "What *can* I do well?" It wasn't false modesty that prevented her answering. She honestly hadn't recognized any of her own abilities.

DISCOVERING AND USING YOUR ABILITIES

There's absolutely no future in thinking or saying, "I can't do anything." One of the most exciting times in a Christian woman's life is when God shows her that she can go beyond what she believes she is capable of doing.

Jeanette Clift George, the actress who portrayed Corrie ten Boom in the movie, "The Hiding Place," said that when she became a Christian she presented two lists to God. One list was titled "Things I Can Do." The other list was titled "Things I Can't Do." She feels certain that as soon as she gave them to God, he got the two lists mixed up. She had no idea when she presented her lists to God that later he would use some of her hidden abilities to reveal more of himself to others.

Moses presented an "I Can't Do" list to God after God told him to go to Pharaoh to demand that he be allowed to lead the Israelites out of Egyptian slavery. His first excuse was, "I can't do it." Next he told God that he wasn't the person for the job. When Moses told God that he had trouble speaking, God answered his excuse by saying, "Moses, don't you realize yet that I'm the one who makes mouths? I can make you to speak or not speak, hear or not hear. Listen to me. I am going to help you speak. I'll even tell you what to say" (author's paraphrase of Exod. 4:11, 12).

I don't recall ever saying "I can't" to God when the doors opened for me to begin a ministry of writing—but I could have been considered one of the most unlikely candidates for the job. All I had in my possession was a stack of daily journals in which I had been writing for over fifteen years.

One day I took the journals out of the closet and began to read them. One sentence had an asterisk by it: *Book idea: "Mom, Take Time." My immediate reaction was, "Writing a book is one of the most ridiculous thoughts I've ever had." I showed the entry to my husband. He didn't think it was ridiculous. He was the one who had encouraged me to start the journals. God had worked through him in that way to guide me toward my future work. As I continued to read the journals I discovered the recurring theme of family living. I had recorded what we did with our children through the years, what I had observed other parents doing with their children, prayers for our children, frustrations with parenting.

After I finished reading through the journals, I knew there was enough material in them to create a book. But I definitely had a problem. All through my years as a student I had never seen the significance of outlining, or of avoiding dangling participles and split infinitives. The only thing about which I was certain was the content I wanted to go into the book.

Two Scripture verses encouraged me throughout the writing. The Bible says, "For when I am weak, then I am strong—the less I have, the more I depend on him" (2 Cor. 12:10b). That verse became personal for me as God turned my weaknesses into strengths—by providing a retired English teacher who was willing to edit my work.

On the days I felt it was ridiculous even to think I had the ability to write a book, God continued to encourage me with a promise from the second special Scripture verse, "God who began the good work within you will keep right on helping you" (Phil. 1:6). My addition to that promise is, "Anytime you feel you lack anything, I will be it for you. Everything you believe you aren't, I AM!"

I finished writing the book in eight months. I put the manuscript in a box, wrapped it, and mailed it to a publisher. It came back. That same day, I wrapped it again and mailed it to another publisher, a procedure I would follow four more times. I would have become discouraged with each new rejection if I had not believed firmly in my mind and heart that God had given me the ability to write. I also believed that some publisher would see the value of my book. Finally, I received an acceptance letter from a publisher.

Six months later a package was delivered to my home. I opened it to find six copies of the delightful finished product—my book, *Mom, Take Time*. I began reading it as though I had never seen it before. I stopped long enough to hold up the book and yell to my husband, "Don, this is really good!"

Since that day, every time I hold a completed manuscript in my hands, I lift it up to God and thank him for giving me the ability to write. That may not sound significant until you know that only a few years ago I felt there was little I could contribute beyond the walls of my home. I believe God picked up on what I considered a weakness, and he transformed "not much, just a stack of journals" into a tool that would bring honor to him.

ONLY A JAR OF OIL

A story is recorded in 2 Kings 4 about a woman who didn't recognize what she possessed until God revealed it to her through the prophet Elisha. When her husband died she was left with two sons and a large debt. She went to Elisha for advice. First, he asked her what she had that might help her pay off the debt. She was probably apologetic or even embarrassed to tell this great man of God that all she had in her possession was a jar of olive oil. This fact didn't deter Elisha. He told her to borrow all the pots and pans she and her sons could find. After they collected all of them, Elisha told the woman to start pouring the small amount of oil into the borrowed pots. Before long, all the containers were filled. She sold the oil, paid her debts, and had enough money left for her and her sons to live on for the rest of their lives. To her, the jar of oil had seemed insignificant—but that was her opinion, not God's.

God sees your beautiful, complex body and he's pleased with the way he created it. He sees the abilities you're using and waits to draw out your other abilities. He asks, "What do you have to give me today?" You might answer, "Lord, I don't have much, but I know that's my opinion, not yours. I've said 'I can't' for so long that I have myself believing I can't do much. I come to you today, just as I am. If anything can be made of me, here I am. I'm at your disposal. I come with all I have."

With this response to God, you are allowing him to help you understand the divine dimension of reverencing and caring for your body. He will use your abilities in ways you never dreamed of. It's going to happen. God promised it!

"Now glory be to God who by his mighty power at work within us is able to do far more than we would ever dare to ask or even dream of— infinitely beyond our highest prayers, desires, thoughts, or hopes" (Eph. 3:20).

🌸 Confronting Yourself

(You may want to spend two discussion periods on this chapter.)

I. During the last twenty-four hours you were to have "fasted" from faultfinding (criticizing). What were the results of your "fast"?
   A. I learned that . . .

   B. I promised that I . . .

II. Sit together in twos and tell your partner how you felt about yourself before you read this chapter. What was the most significant truth you learned from this chapter?

III. Read 1 Corinthians 6:19, 20 from different
translations. After you have contemplated this truth:
A. Paraphrase the verses in your own words.

B. Find the key word.

C. Choose the phrase that confirms your
importance to God.

D. Relate these verses to your life at this time.

IV. Considering the truth in 1 Corinthians 6:19, 20,
confront yourself with the following self-
examination.
A. What are some self-defeating thoughts you've
lived with through the years that have pertained
to your physical makeup? As you recall
nicknames, teasing, "putdowns" by family
members and others, as well as thoughts you've
imposed upon yourself, list them here.

B. Study your list. Are some of these things still painful to you? If so, why? What options do you have to get rid of them?

V. Name some messages you give your body that say: "I love you."

"I don't love you."

Be specific. Include relaxation or the lack of it; eating properly or improperly; exercising regularly, sometimes, never.

VI. Draw a simple outline of a woman. On the outline check the part(s) of your body you have trouble accepting. Is there something you can do to change it? If so, set down some goals that will bring about the change. Share these goals with one other person in the group. Become a support team to help each other reach these goals.

SHORT-TERM GOALS   **LONG-TERM GOALS**

VII. Tell one person in your group something you admire about her personal appearance.

VIII. Using the truth from Romans 12:3, "Be honest in your estimate of yourselves," finish this sentence: "I'm good at _____." If it takes you more than thirty seconds to think of something, ask your group to help you be aware of some of those things you do well. If you were able to respond, share that ability with one other person in the group. If you feel comfortable with your group, encourage each person to share within the group.

IX. Using Romans 12:6a, "God has given each of us the ability to do certain things well" answer these questions:

A. What is the key word?

B. What promise is in this verse?

C. What might keep you from claiming this promise?

X. The following abilities are listed in Romans 12:7, 8:

A. Serving others

B. Studying/teaching

C. Making and using money to help others

D. Using administrative abilities

E. Offering comfort

Which of these abilities have you been given?

Be more specific about these abilities and give a verbal "gift" to one of the women in your group by telling her which ability you believe she possesses.

XI. Write something you have always wanted to do because you know you have the ability, but have never done. Do not sign your name. Collect and mix the papers. Redistribute the papers to the group. Ask the women to read these "dreams" aloud and give the other women the opportunity to guess who wrote them. If you are not in a group, write your dream here.

After you have claimed your "dream," share with the group or write here what arrangements you would have to make for your dream to come true. Form support teams and take the necessary steps to fulfill your dream. Check on each other weekly to see if the goals are being reached.

XII. "God has been made rich because we who are Christ's have been given to him" (Eph. 1:18).
A. What is the spiritual truth?

B. What does this verse say to you personally?

XIII. *RESOLVE* to offer up your body and abilities to God.

Each day this week, give some person a genuine compliment or express your love in an unexpected way. (Remember: family members aren't exempt.)

Record each person's reaction (positive/negative).

Notice if your words or actions brought any change in the person's life or *yours!*

S T R E T C H I N G

E X E R C I S E S

*Open my eyes to see wonderful things in
your Word.*

FIRST DAY:
*"You made all the delicate, inner parts of my body, and
knit them together in my mother's womb. Thank you for
making me so wonderfully complex! It is amazing to think
about. Your workmanship is marvelous—and how well I
know it. You were there while I was being formed in utter
seclusion! You saw me before I was born and scheduled
each day of my life before I began to breathe"* (Ps.
139:13-15).

SECOND DAY:
*"Haven't you yet learned that your body is the home of
the Holy Spirit God gave you, and that he lives within
you? Your own body does not belong to you. For God has
bought you with a great price. So use every part of your
body to give glory back to God, because he owns it"*
(1 Cor. 6:19, 20).

THIRD DAY:
*"We Christians actually do have within us a portion of
the very thoughts and mind of Christ"* (1 Cor. 2:16b).

FOURTH DAY:
*"Be sure to use the abilities God has given you. . . . Put
these abilities to work; throw yourself into your tasks so*

that everyone may notice your improvement and progress" (1 Tim. 4:14, 15).

FIFTH DAY:
"Once you were [past tense] less than nothing; now you are [present tense] God's own. Once you knew very little of God's kindness; now your very lives have been changed by it" (1 Pet. 2:10).

SIXTH DAY:
"I want you to realize that God has been made rich because we who are Christ's have been given to him!" (Eph. 1:18b).

SEVENTH DAY:
"And since we are his children, we will share his treasures—for all God gives to his Son Jesus is now ours too" (Rom. 8:17).

ADVANCED STRETCHING EXERCISE
"Now glory be to God who by his mighty power at work within us is able to do far more than we would ever dare to ask or even dream of—infinitely beyond our highest prayers, desires, thoughts, or hopes" (Eph. 3:20).

6
Ministering Like Jesus

The first five truths have presented valuable
insights about God and yourself. They have been
gradually preparing you for the final truth: You are
called to minister to people the way Jesus
ministered to them. This truth involves three
principles: (1) seeing people the way Jesus saw
them; (2) loving people the way Jesus loved them;
and (3) demonstrating Jesus' love to people.

THE FIRST PRINCIPLE

It is difficult to see people the way Jesus saw them
because "Man looketh on the outward appearance"
(1 Sam. 16:7, KJV). It's hard to go beyond people's
outward appearances since we live in a culture
that values personal color analysis, up-to-the-
minute fashion trends, fit, beautiful bodies, and
wrinkle-free skin. Following these earth-bound
standards, it's easy to develop first impressions of
people based on their outward appearances.

If you were to observe the outward appearance

of one of my friends you would notice his strong, rugged physique, beautiful graying hair, and a determined, square jaw. If that surface glance were all you took in, you couldn't know the depth of his anguish over the untimely death of his wife.

If you could see another one of my friends you would immediately notice her flawless olive skin, the right shades and amounts of makeup, and a beautiful smile. Her tasteful clothing flatters her figure. But if you perceived beyond her outward appearance you would find that her heart was breaking because her husband has fallen in love with another woman.

Observing another friend, you would notice her lovely hands, puffy eyes, and a stooped back. Her forced smile would not allow you to see that she had been experiencing a deep depression for many months.

As I stand before groups of women at conferences, the first things I notice might be their sizes, hairstyles, makeup, or clothing. Before these meetings are over I learn that many of them have recently gained victories over heartbreaking circumstances and others are still in the middle of difficult situations. These women are dealing with financial reverses, serious illnesses of family members, damaged marriages, devastating relationships with their teens, loneliness following a move to a new location, or problems at work. Their outward appearances seldom reflect the turmoil of their inner selves, the secret part that cries out to have someone see and understand what's happening and minister to them.

Jesus saw people differently. The conclusion of 1 Samuel 16:7 says that God looks at the heart. Jesus went beyond outward appearances to perceive people's needs. He mixed with people

whom the Pharisees considered "scum." He saw
into the heart of the Samaritan woman at the well
and recognized her special need. When Jesus saw
Zacchaeus his first impression wasn't, "That's the
shortest man I've ever seen!" Jesus saw not only a
man who had climbed up into a tree, but one who
needed what Jesus could give him.

What impression would you have had of John the
Baptist? You might have noticed that he talked
loudly, to the point of being obnoxious. It wouldn't
take a long look to learn that he didn't dress in the
latest fashions. We probably would have labeled
him "socially unacceptable." But Jesus saw the
heart of John the Baptist and could say, "Truly, I
say to you, among those born of women there has
not arisen anyone greater than John the Baptist"
(Matt. 11:11, NASB). He saw a prophet who would
be "one of the Lord's great men" (Luke 1:15).

If it had been left to us, we would have marked
off our list the woman who already had five
husbands and was living with a man she hadn't
bothered to marry. By the way she looked and
lived, we would have known that she wasn't "one
of us." But Jesus saw her heart. He saw a sinner
who wanted his help, who wanted to know how to
live.

The Scriptures say nothing about the outward
appearance of the thief on the cross. Jesus looked
beyond his appearance and past his mistakes to see
a man who needed and wanted his blessing.

Jesus was a master at looking beyond people's
outward appearances. By example he kept saying,
"Look at me." "Watch closely." "This is the way you
are to see people." Whether it was because of his
touch or the words he spoke, the people who
responded to him were never the same again.

With Jesus' life providing so many visual aids,

why are we so slow to follow his examples? It should be obvious that outward appearances tell so little and that our first impressions are often wrong. These two facts make it imperative that we learn the kind of discernment which takes us beyond people's outward appearances and gives us glimpses of their hearts.

THE SECOND PRINCIPLE

The second biblical principle involves loving people the way Jesus loved them. Jesus presented this truth when he commanded us to "love each other just as much as I love you" (John 13:34b) and to "love your neighbor as much as you love yourself" (Matt. 22:39).

Jesus loved Lazarus so much that the Jews commented, "See! how tenderly he loved him!" (John 11:36, Rhm.). He kept loving the rich young ruler even after he rejected what Jesus could give him. Jesus' love for his mother was apparent during his crucifixion as he made provision for John to care for Mary after he was gone. Jesus' love was so great that he could forgive the men who were putting him to death.

Jesus' examples of loving stimulate us to love others. During a women's conference one of the workshop leaders instructed those in the group to look around the room and find one person whom they loved but had never told. They were instructed to go to that person, hug her, and say nothing. Within seconds the women began moving everywhere, hugging each other, but completely ignoring their instructions.

They were expressing how much they loved and appreciated each other. Some were laughing, others were crying. Their pastor was standing in the hall outside the room as the conference ended. The women left the room and many of them hugged this unsuspecting man and told him that they loved him. Later he asked, "What in the world was going on in that room?" Obviously for a moment these women were following the command to "love one another."

It's easy to love people who return our love, but it is difficult to love people who have stumbled and made mistakes. Shortly after I arrived home from a trip I learned that a friend was in serious trouble. Some in the Christian community were making her problem more difficult by being critical and ignoring her. I called her and arranged to have lunch with her. As we ate, she told me about her mistake and added that she and her family were trying to work things out. Then she looked at me and said, "I'm so glad you aren't ashamed to be seen with me."

I cupped her face in my hands and said, "I love you as much now as I loved you before you made this mistake. You must believe me." She said she did. We had other special times after that day.

That firsthand experience taught me a lesson that I pray will last a lifetime: to look *beyond* the mistakes of others and to love them, as much as I can, as Jesus loved them.

It's an indication that this second principle is becoming a way of life for you when you refrain from repeating vicious words you would have been so ready to whisper before. Loving people the way Jesus loved them definitely requires a "renewing of your mind" (Rom. 12:2a, KJV), a new conscience that allows you to love people who may not always respond to your love.

THE THIRD PRINCIPLE

As you see people the way Jesus saw them and love them the way Jesus loved them, you are ready for the third principle: demonstrating Jesus' kind of love. This gives you a deliberate consciousness to want to demonstrate that love to others. The Scriptures say, "Stop just *saying* [you] love people . . . *really* love them and *show it* by [your] actions" (1 John 3:18).

Throughout the Gospels it seems that Jesus never commanded us to do anything that he wasn't willing to do himself. When Jesus taught about love he proceeded to exemplify it. Jesus demonstrated his love for the woman whom the Pharisees were ready to stone. He stood by her and caused the men to disperse by saying, "Let the sinless man among you be the first to throw a stone at her" (John 8:7b, Wey.). The sound of the stones dropping at the Pharisees' feet surely demonstrated to the woman the fearlessness of Jesus' love.

In another instance his love was demonstrated to a suffering woman who believed that all she had to do to be cured of her illness was to touch the hem of Jesus' garment. When Jesus turned and saw who had purposely touched his robe, he had no thought of rebuking her. Instead, he announced to her in front of the crowd, "Daughter . . . all is well! Your faith has healed you" (Matt. 9:22).

There is a cost in demonstrating Jesus' love. Time is the major part of it. Some acts of love may require only two or three minutes. Other ministries will totally demolish your daily routine, happen at the most inconvenient times, delay your personal goals, or generate tremendous anguish. But even those costs aren't too much when you understand Jesus' teaching, "Inasmuch as ye have done it unto one of the least of these my brethren, ye have done it unto me" (Matt. 25:40b, KJV).

It would be foolish to waste time trying to decide whether an outward expression of love is necessary or unnecessary, great or small. Jesus said to be ready for even the "small" acts (Matt. 25:21a, NEB).

Instead of forming a committee to decide who, how, why, when, or where people should give compliments, simply start doing it. Giving a genuine compliment to at least one person per day is no "small" act. "I appreciate you." "You're doing a great job." (Employers and parents, take note.) "You ministered to me." These are all one-second, one-line compliments that most people could live on for a week after receiving.

The world has become too silent; people rarely compliment each other or say "I love you." Either people have fallen into the habit of not taking the time to give compliments or else they have considered them as "small" for so long that "it doesn't matter whether we give them or not."

A young mother told a group of women how the relationship with her daughter changed after she complimented her daughter on the way she had cleaned the kitchen. She and her daughter had exchanged few decent words and even fewer physical contacts for several months. The night after the teenager received her timely compliment, she put her arms around her mother and told her that she loved her.

When a compliment has the potential of changing the relationship between a mother and her teen, it isn't "small." The writer of Proverbs says, "a word of encouragement does wonders!" (Prov. 12:25).

Jesus said we are to love each other as much as

he loves us. Since this command offers us no
option, why do we neglect to demonstrate our love
toward others? Have you ever wondered why you
hesitate to tell your husband how much you love
him for playing with the children, keeping the cars
in good running condition, or fixing his own
breakfast so you can sleep later?

Are you aware that very few people stop young
parents and tell them that they're doing a great job
as mothers and dads? Has it been a long time since
you've expressed your love to your parents for the
ways they've helped you when you were having a
hard time financially?

The third principle embraces the idea of
practicing awareness of the needs of others and
doing something about them—until it becomes
second nature to you. This practice eliminates the
neglect of good intentions.

Diligently practicing Jesus' love will keep you
from ignoring the "invisible generation"—those
saintly people seventy years and older. You will
take time to let them know that they still occupy
an important space on this planet! You'll ask them
to sit with you when you see them sitting alone at
church or in other public places. You'll invite the
widows and widowers into your home because you
can imagine how lonely it must be for them to eat
every meal by themselves. You'll hug them more
often, knowing how they must miss being hugged
by their mates.

Practicing your love puts restraints on playing
your private game of "The Great Pretender."
Women sometimes play it at the grocery store.
Picture this scene: You've rushed to the grocery
store to get the necessary ingredients for the
evening meal. You're racing up and down the aisles
and you see a friend before she sees you. But

remember, you're in a hurry and you can't afford to get caught in conversation. So you bury your head in the fresh produce or the dairy case and pretend you don't see her because you don't have time to talk. A danger with this game is that she may be the person who needs your love that day.

Demonstrating love will not only stop you from complaining about your doctor bill, it may encourage you to go the second mile by sending a thank-you note to your doctor for helping you or a family member through an illness. You may want to express appreciation for his prescribing the right treatment and taking time to assure you that everything was going to be all right. Until you start demonstrating your love you probably will feel that getting your payment in on time is sufficient.

There's a long list of professionals who serve you faithfully. Demonstrating Jesus' love to them may mean going past the "paid in full" and verbally acknowledging your gratefulness.

God has been generous to give me friends whose thoughtful acts of love serve to exemplify his love. Some friends have had flowers delivered to my home when they learned I had experienced a disappointment or was lonely.

I have awakened from surgery to find the windowsill crowded with flowers and a stack of cards by my bed. There were friends who drove a long distance to attend my father-in-law's funeral. I can still remember the feeling I had when I saw them there. And then they sent a tree to be planted in memory of the father who had defended, protected, and loved my husband all those years.

There have been self-appointed committees of women who brought food and cleaned my house the first week after each of my daughters was born. Our special lifelong friends remembered many of our wedding anniversaries and showed up to care for our children so my husband and I could have an evening out together. And unsung heroines hosted our grown daughters' weddings and baby showers.

We've had neighbors who shared fresh trout and vegetables with us, invited us into their homes for meals, and volunteered to care for our house and lawn while we were on vacation. There have been the silent ones who sent notes of encouragement which arrived at just the right time, and still others who chose to remain anonymous in their demonstrations of love.

My parents have exhibited some of the truest forms of love. On several occasions they have slipped money into my purse during our lean years. I recall Mother hiding an iron in my suitcase when she saw the condition of my iron, and Dad taking my car and filling the gas tank before my trip home. Both of them demonstrated the kind of love in their marriage that I always wanted to have in mine. Special expressions of love continue to be shown through their lives and in the lives of my husband and children. Being a recipient of such love has enriched my life and I find that I want to love others as I have been loved.

Jesus knows that certain demonstrations of love require longer time involvements and higher levels of stress. These are the relationships in which God chooses for you to express such an intensity of love toward someone that you must continually cry out to him in prayer for help. He has witnessed your faithfulness in what you might consider to be small acts, and now you're prepared for the greater ones.

Some of the "greater" demands have called me to spend hours with a friend who was informed by her doctor that her daughter had a malignancy. I saw the hopelessness in her eyes and wondered why she couldn't cry.

I have gone into the hospital room of a young mother who lost her baby at birth, sat in silence with her, and dried her tears and mine.

A greater calling also might send you to a neighbor's house after a phone call and lead you to wrap your arms around a brand new widow.

You may end up crying with parents whose teen, voted by his classmates as "most likely to succeed," has committed suicide.

Several years ago I discipled a young woman whom I believed had the "perfect" marriage. She intimidated me at times because of her voluntary submissiveness to her husband. One day she stopped by my house. I can remember her coming in, sitting down, and saying nothing for a few minutes—an unusual procedure for both of us. Then she announced that her husband was leaving her and proceeded to tell me why.

As she talked I felt a mixture of anger and empathy. I felt hatred toward the power that Satan uses to ruin marriages, and hurt for a young couple who had honestly intended to spend the rest of their lives together.

Something had happened unexpectedly and their sacred vows had been broken. She sent her children to her mother's house to shield them from some of the hurting, and she spent several nights in our home. She shared openly how the brokenness was affecting the children, her husband, and herself.

We cried together. We even made plans to "get even" with her husband. But toward the end of their ordeal we cried and prayed for him. He was hurting, too.

Several weeks later she knocked at my kitchen door. She fell into my arms and cried, "It's all over."

The greater involvements we have in others' lives can hurt unmercifully. Sometimes there are no appropriate words to say. When you try to say them, they sound empty. You wonder what you can do.

You finally read some Scripture verses and the sustaining power of God's Word tells you to weep unashamedly with those who weep (Rom. 12:15, NASB). As the full realization of what has happened begins to hit you, you cry.

Later, you write a note to that one who is hurting. You try to think of a gift that you might take to visually express your love, or you bake a cake to deliver because you don't know what else to do.

Your heart is already telling you that it's going to take more than delivering the cake, writing a note, or giving a gift. No matter what you have scheduled over the next several weeks, you'll spend some of the most unselfish days you've ever spent, demonstrating the cost that's involved in loving people the way Jesus loved them.

Of all the truths that have been discovered in God's Word, the ultimate one is God's demonstration of love. "But God demonstrates His own love toward us, in that while we were yet sinners, Christ died for us" (Rom. 5:8, NASB).

From the beginning, even before his Master Plan began, it was God's love that would send Jesus to us, to die for us, in order that we might personally taste eternal life. In his short lifetime on earth, God's Son lived out each example of love supremely and perfectly according to the Father's original design—and that perfect plan is to be continued through you and me.

"You have not chosen Me, but I have chosen you—I have appointed you, I have planted you— that you might go and bear fruit and keep on bearing; that your fruit may be lasting (that it may remain . . .)" (John 15:16, Amp.).

Confronting Yourself

I. Assignment Report
   A. Last week you were asked to give a compliment
      or say "I love you" to a different person each day.
      What were some of their reactions?

      "I learned that . . ."

      "I promised myself that . . ."

   B. Share a compliment someone gave you this week
      and tell how it made you feel.

II. Confronting Yourself
   A. How have you usually ministered to the needs
      of . . . ?
      1. a new mother

2. a widow/widower
3. a recent divorcee
4. a seriously ill person
5. a new family in town/neighborhood
6. a lonely person
7. a friend who has lost his/her job
8. an "impossible" employer/child/in-law (With this one, remember, with God *all* things are possible.)

Believing God when he commanded that "you must always treat other people as you would like to have them treat you" (Matt. 7:12, Gspd.), how should you minister to the people listed above?

B. Tell one person in the group how you have ministered to someone in an unusual way, or share something special someone has done for you.

III. How would these verses prepare you for a greater ministry?
   A. Luke 10:38-42

B. Matthew 6:19

C. John 1:41

D. John 13:4, 5

E. Luke 9:23-25

IV. Look at each resolution you have made near the end of each "Confronting Yourself" section.
A. Which ones have you accomplished?

B. Which ones still need some work?

C. What new goals do you believe God would have you to pursue?

V. These past weeks you have read and discussed:
   A. that God's truths are available to everyone
   B. some basics God included within his Master Plan
   C. a faith that grows from listening to God through the Scriptures
   D. God's plan for complete forgiveness
   E. God's pleasure in the way he created your body and gave you abilities
   F. ministering to people the way Jesus ministered to them

Considering what you have learned from this book and the group discussions, what do you expect God to do with your life in some of these areas? Write your expectations.

In prayer, give these expectations to God as your gift to him. What he chooses to do with your expectations, accept as his gift to you.

VI. SHARING
   A. Go quietly to one other person in your group. Hold her hand. Share one area of your life that has been affected since this study began. After that one has listened, she will place her hands on your head and pray that this change will grow and bring honor to God.

B. Write who or what you believe you are holding in your hand that needs to be offered to God in order for him to make you the woman he wants you to be. Offer that person or thing to God while everyone prays silently.

C. Say in unison: "May I never forget your words; for they are my only hope. Therefore I will keep on obeying you forever and forever, free within the limits of your law" (Ps. 119:43-45).

S T R E T C H I N G
E X E R C I S E S

Open my eyes to see wonderful things in
your Word.

FIRST DAY:
"Are you called to help others? Do it with all the strength
and energy that God supplies, so that God will be
glorified through Jesus Christ" (1 Pet. 4:11b).

SECOND DAY:
"Share each other's troubles and problems, and so obey
our Lord's command. If anyone thinks he is too great to
stoop to this, he is fooling himself" (Gal. 6:2, 3).

THIRD DAY:
"In response to all he has done for us, let us outdo each
other in being helpful and kind to each other and in
doing good" (Heb. 10:24).

FOURTH DAY:
"Do you think you deserve credit for merely loving those
who love you? Even the godless do that! And if you do
good only to those who do you good—is that so
wonderful? Even sinners do that much!" (Luke 6:32, 33).

FIFTH DAY:
"But prove yourselves doers of the word, and not merely
hearers who delude themselves. For if anyone is a hearer
of the word and not a doer, he is like a man who looks at
his natural face in a mirror; for once he has looked at

himself and gone away, he has immediately forgotten what kind of person he was. But one who looks intently at the perfect law, the law of liberty, and abides by it, not having become a forgetful hearer but an effectual doer, this man shall be blessed in what he does" (James 1:22-25, NASB).

SIXTH DAY:
"It is God himself who has made us what we are and given us new lives from Christ Jesus; and long ages ago he planned that we should spend these lives in helping others" (Eph. 2:10).

SEVENTH DAY:
"And so, as those who have been chosen of God, holy and beloved, put on a heart of compassion, kindness, humility, gentleness and patience" (Col. 3:12, NASB).

ADVANCED STRETCHING EXERCISE
"Feed the flock of God; care for it willingly, not grudgingly; not for what you will get out of it, but because you are eager to serve the Lord" (1 Pet. 5:2).